QUEEN ELIZABETH II AND HER CHURCH

QUEEN ELIZABETH II AND HER CHURCH

Royal Service at Westminster Abbey

JOHN HALL

Dean of Westminster

B L O O M S B U R Y   C O N T I N U U M

LONDON • OXFORD • NEW YORK • NEW DELHI • SYDNEY

BLOOMSBURY CONTINUUM
Bloomsbury Publishing Plc
50 Bedford Square, London, WC1B 3DP, UK
29 Earlsfort Terrace, Dublin 2, Ireland

BLOOMSBURY, BLOOMSBURY CONTINUUM and the Diana logo are
trademarks of Bloomsbury Publishing Plc

First published in Great Britain 2012
This edition published 2022

A catalogue record for this book is available from the British Library

Library of Congress Cataloguing-in-Publication data has been applied for

ISBN: 978-1-3994-0940-7

2 4 6 8 10 9 7 5 3 1

Typeset by Deanta Global Publishing Services, Chennai, India
Printed and bound in Great Britain by CPI Group (UK) Ltd, Croydon CR0 4YY

To find out more about our authors and books visit www.bloomsbury.com
and sign up for our newsletters

CONTENTS

Introduction

This book is about Westminster Abbey as Queen Elizabeth II's church. It is also about servant leadership, the leadership exercised by Jesus Christ. Such leadership is an example and model for the leadership the Queen exercises. It must also be a model for the leadership we ourselves exercise.

Westminster Abbey is a place of captivating interest: the coronation church, where English kings and queens have been anointed and crowned since 1066, where Queen Elizabeth II was crowned on 2 June 1953; the Queen's church, known as a Royal Peculiar, where royal weddings and funerals are held and where the Queen and other members of the Royal Family attend special services and celebrations every year.

This book celebrates Christian values. Westminster Abbey stands for clear Christian values and for stability in a changing world. The values of our civilization, of Britain and of the English-speaking world, have been firmly based on Christian belief and the Christian story. But as that story has become gradually less well known and understood and the beliefs associated with it have been less firmly grasped, so too the values to which it has given rise have become less coherently understood and perceived. Celebrating and proclaiming those values is an important part of the Abbey's mission.

The Abbey's daily round of worship and of welcoming visitors is punctured by special services, often attended by the Queen or another member of the Royal Family. This book tells the story of some of these special services, most of which have taken place within my first five years as Dean of Westminster. I describe why and how we have conducted these special services, each of which is fascinating in itself. And each one I connect to the values honoured and celebrated in the service in question. I also fill out the picture, weaving in accounts of the history and contemporary life of the Abbey.

At the head of each chapter I flag up the fruits of the Spirit as described by St Paul, as a means of identifying the values to which I refer: love, joy, peace, forbearance, kindness, generosity, faithfulness, gentleness and self-control. A servant leader will demonstrate the fruits of the Spirit: will be loving, joyful, peaceful, forbearing, kind, generous, faithful, gentle and self-controlling. At the end of each chapter, I include a prayer, relating to the particular event I am describing, a prayer which is used in the Abbey. I hope they will enrich the experience of reading this book and assist in reflection on the duty and privilege of service.

The book starts with the Coronation of Her Majesty Queen Elizabeth II in 1953. I describe the service itself in some detail but I also have a point to make. Let me put it this way. The essence of the coronation has been unchanging over the centuries, though much of the detail has changed. At its heart, the anointing of the Sovereign, and the clothing with priestly garments that precede the coronation itself, resemble the ordination of a priest or the consecration of a bishop. The coronation is a setting apart for service after the pattern of Jesus Christ.

Jesus said, 'The Son of Man came not to be served but to serve and to give his life a ransom for many.' (Mark 10:45) This idea of royal service does have a guiding place at the heart of the story of civilization. It can be seen most clearly at the coronation, one of the high points of self-expression of the values underlying our island story.

Queen Elizabeth II came to the throne on 6 February 1952, so 2012 marks her diamond jubilee. This book is a celebration of part of one aspect of her remarkable life of commitment and duty, dedicated to the service of almighty God, of the nation and of the Commonwealth. The Queen is rightly recognized and honoured throughout the world. Serving the Queen, being in royal service, is a privilege.

1

Anointing and Coronation

'The fruit of the Spirit is love, joy, peace, forbearance, kindness, generosity, faithfulness, gentleness and self-control' (Galatians 5: 22).

Joy

I was four at the time. It is one of my earliest memories. I was sitting with my parents, sister and brothers and various aunts around my grandparents' eight-inch television screen, peering intently at a flickering black-and-white image. Now in an age of wide-screen high-definition colour television, it seems almost incredible that we saw anything. But there we were, eagerly watching the coronation of Queen Elizabeth II. I remember a great sense of occasion, and a spirit of veneration, even of awe.

Countless family groups up and down the country were just like us, many of them watching TV sets newly acquired for the purpose. But this was much more than a moment in television history. It was a great royal ceremony, one to catch the eye and the imagination, with glitter, pomp and magnificence. George VI's coronation in 1937 had been filmed for the cinema. Now for the first time, people had immediate access through the television to what was happening at the time. We could all feel we had some part in it. But I wonder how far the complex ceremonies and the rolling phrases in sixteenth-century English spoke to the audience in the Abbey, let alone in our homes, of what it all stood for, what it all meant.

Now that I am living and working at the Abbey, I have had a chance to sort things out in my own mind. For example, I have now seen exactly where the Coronation Chair was placed and which way it faced. I had scarcely given the question which way it faced a thought before I came to the Abbey, but I remember discovering to my surprise that the Chair faces the high altar. The Queen was crowned with her back to the congregation. Even the throne, high up in what I have discovered is called the coronation theatre, faces the altar. I suppose it should be obvious, but I had somehow assumed that the ceremony of coronation would be performed so that as many people as possible could see. In fact, there is a degree of privacy, of intimacy at the heart of the ceremony. The Sovereign faces the high altar, the most sacred part of the Abbey, just like the couple at a wedding ceremony. At a coronation, the engagement is between the Sovereign and God. That is the key relationship. The people have their role in the service, giving their assent at the beginning and later paying homage, but the exchange is between the Sovereign and God. The Sovereign offers an oath of loyalty and service. God offers the gift of grace and the anointing of the Holy Spirit. It is a mutual exchange of gifts, the Queen offering to serve God and her people and God offering in return to bless and uphold her.

There is ample public evidence that for Queen Elizabeth II at her coronation on 2 June 1953, this offering of service was well understood. On her 21st birthday, the then Princess Elizabeth broadcast from South Africa a radio message to the people of the United Kingdom and the Commonwealth. She pledged herself then to commit her whole life 'whether it be long or short' to duty and service. She deliberately spoke in the most solemn words about going forward together 'with an unwavering faith, a high courage, and a quiet heart'. Her aim was that the Commonwealth should be a 'powerful influence for good in the world':

> To accomplish that we must give nothing less than the whole of ourselves. There is a motto which has been borne by many of my ancestors – a noble motto, 'I serve'. I declare before you all that my whole life whether it be long or short shall be devoted to your service. But I shall not have strength to carry out this resolution alone unless you join in it with me, as I now invite you to do: I know that your support will be unfailingly given. God help me to make good my vow, and God bless all of you who are willing to share in it.

The Queen spoke in a similar way in a broadcast on the evening of her coronation:

> Throughout this memorable day I have been uplifted and sustained by the knowledge that your thoughts and prayers were with me. It is hard for me to find words in which to tell you of the strength which this knowledge has given me.
>
> The ceremonies you have seen today are ancient, and some of their origins are veiled in the mists of the past. But their spirit and their meaning shine through the ages never, perhaps, more brightly than now. I have in sincerity pledged myself to your service, as so

many of you are pledged to mine. Throughout all my life and with all my heart I shall strive to be worthy of your trust.

Sixty years later the words ring as true as they did when they were first spoken, and nothing has occurred that would cause anyone to doubt the sincerity of the commitment that lay behind them or the strength of the faith and confidence in God's call and anointing with which they were imbued.

I hope that by going into some of the details of the service itself in this chapter, I can show how the Coronation expresses with absolute clarity the fundamental values the monarchy represents, values which I am summing up in the phrase *servant leadership*, about which I shall say more later. It is worth reflecting that the Coronation service is not reinvented each time but follows a powerful tradition which has been sustained at the Abbey down the centuries. Every one of the key elements has remained present in the service through good times and bad, with sovereigns whose reign appeared to promise peace and prosperity and with sovereigns whose reign filled their contemporaries with dread.

One of the most precious objects in the Abbey's archives is a fourteenth-century illuminated manuscript called the *Liber regalis*. This beautiful little book is an instruction manual for coronations and claims tenth-century authority. So the way a king or queen has been crowned in England has been unchanging in its essentials for well over a thousand years. In the *Liber regalis* are three forms of service for coronations: of a king; of a queen consort; and of a king and queen together. The last Saxon king Harold was crowned in the Abbey on 6 January 1066. The first Norman king, William I (the Conqueror), was crowned in the Abbey on Christmas Day that same year. Since then, all three versions of the coronation have been used at different times. Sometimes a king was married already when he came to the throne and his queen was crowned with him. On other occasions, a king was single and crowned alone. When he subsequently married, his queen had her own coronation, a ceremony that presumably became rather familiar to Henry VIII. There was no provision in the fourteenth-century for the reign of a queen. No queen had ever been crowned who reigned alone, nor would any until Mary I in 1553 and her sister Elizabeth I in 1558. As queens regnant, they were crowned using the form for a king. The three key elements of the service remain: the sovereign's oath; the anointing; the crowning. They are always set within the context of the celebration of Holy Communion.

Queen Elizabeth II's coronation, the fourth in the twentieth century, took place on 2 June 1953, over a year after her accession to the throne on 6 February 1952. Those months of the Queen's reign saw energetic preparations for the great event. These included the transformation of the Abbey during almost a year's closure to visitors, which must have been an immensely strange and costly experience for the Abbey community. A wooden floor was laid over the stone floor of the Abbey and rail tracks laid down to allow building materials to be introduced. At the lantern crossing, where the north–south axis of the transepts meets the west–east main axis of the church, the Theatre was levelled with the Sacrarium itself, the space in front of the high altar, and an additional tier of steps lifted the Queen's throne above the level of the coronation chair in the middle of the Sacrarium. Great tiers of seating in galleries were erected in the north and south transepts and around the quire and in the nave. It is possible to set out on the floor of the Abbey just over two thousand seats without putting at risk people's ability to move around safely. The additional tiers of seating, on great scaffolds going very high under the ceiling, created enough space to accommodate 8,000 people in the Abbey. I find it hard to imagine the experience of being stuck high up under the ceiling for several hours. It must also have taken ages to get everyone in and out. Peeresses secreted sandwiches in their coronets.

The tension must have been considerable as the moment for the Queen's entrance came closer. It was broken when someone came in with a carpet sweeper for the red carpet down the middle of the Abbey. Finally, the moment came with a heralding fanfare of trumpets.

The Queen's entrance was marked, as at every coronation since 1902, by the choir singing Psalm 122 set to music by Sir Hubert Parry. The psalm was most probably written to celebrate the triumphal entry of the king and the people of God in ancient Israel into the capital city, the great city of Zion, Jerusalem, so revered by Jews, Christians and Muslims, and often understood as a powerful image of heaven. The psalm includes a prayer for peace and prosperity.

I was glad when they said unto me:
We will go into the house of the Lord.
Our feet shall stand in thy gates:
O Jerusalem.
Jerusalem is built as a city:
that is at unity in itself.
O pray for the peace of Jerusalem:
they shall prosper that love thee.
Peace be within thy walls:
and plenteousness within thy palaces.

The forty Queen's Scholars of Westminster School have a historic right to shout *Vivat Rex* or *Vivat Regina* at the coronation: *Long live the King* or *Long live the Queen*. Parry modified the shout into a tuneful addition to the music of the anthem: *vivat, vivat, vivat Regina Elizabetha*. The anthem has been immensely popular over the past century and is frequently sung at services of all kinds, including a royal wedding. But the Vivats, which are inserted before the injunction to pray for the peace of Jerusalem, are only ever sung at celebrations of the Coronation in the presence of the Sovereign.

During the anthem, after her entry, the Queen moved to a chair on the south side of the Sacrarium and knelt in private prayer. Her prayer desk was just in front of the royal box, set up a little higher, where her mother and sister, Queen Elizabeth The Queen Mother and Princess Margaret, would later be accompanied by her children, Prince Charles and Princess Anne.

Then came the 'Recognition': a moment that reflects ancient history. When William the Conqueror died there was no certainty who would be the next king – a son, but which? William II, better known as William Rufus, was the Conqueror's third son, and *his* successor, Henry I, the fourth son. Almost three centuries later, at the coronation on 13 October 1399 of Henry Bolingbroke who had deposed Richard II to reign as Henry IV, this recognition must have been a moment of confirmation. For certain subsequent monarchs too – as late as the seventeenth and eighteenth centuries – the succession was by no means uncontested. About Queen Elizabeth II's right to the throne there was of course no doubt whatever. The Archbishop with the Lord Chancellor and Earl Marshal led the Queen to the four sides of the Coronation

Theatre for the Recognition by the people, who responded with *God save Queen Elizabeth.*

Now that she had been recognized as Queen, the next step was for the Archbishop to administer the oath. The terms of the oath have changed over the centuries. Above all, the oath is a solemn promise to rule justly under God and to maintain the position of the Church, of the Christian faith at the heart of the nation. The position of the Established Church has been under attack for centuries, so the terms of the oath have been a matter of discussion. I learnt as a young boy that the longest word in the English language was *antidisestablishmentarianism.* The word was coined in the nineteenth century, when strong positions were being taken for and against the establishment of the Church of England, for and against its position as *state church.* Those who subscribed to *antidisestablishmentarianism* were opposed to the disestablishment of the Church and wanted to maintain things as they were. In the coronation oath the Queen promised to do just that. It is worth quoting in full.

> Will you solemnly promise and swear to govern the Peoples of the United Kingdom of Great Britain and Northern Ireland, Canada, Australia, New Zealand, the Union of South Africa, Pakistan and Ceylon, and of your Possessions and other Territories to any of them belonging or pertaining, according to their respective laws and customs?
>
> I solemnly promise so to do.
>
> Will you to your power cause Law and Justice, in Mercy, to be executed in all your judgements?
>
> I will.

Will you to the utmost of your power maintain the Laws of God and the true profession of the Gospel?

Will you to the utmost of your power maintain in the United Kingdom the Protestant Reformed Religion established by law?

Will you maintain and preserve inviolably the settlement of the Church of England, and the doctrine, worship, discipline, and government thereof, as by law established in England?

And will you preserve unto the Bishops and Clergy of England, and to the Churches there committed to their charge, all such rights and privileges, as by law do or shall appertain to them or any of them?

All this I promise to do.

Laying her hand on the Bible, the Queen confirmed her oath, saying: 'The things which I have here promised, I will perform, and keep. So help me God.'

The preliminaries over, it was time to begin the service of Holy Communion from the Church of England's Book of Common Prayer, as it was restored by Charles II in 1662, with the Collect for Purity and the Collect for the service, including a petition that, in her time as Queen, Christian devotion might continue in peace.

Two biblical readings emphasized the Christian commitment to serve God as well as the State, represented by the Monarch: 'Render unto Caesar the things which are Caesar's and unto God the things that are God's.' The congregation then professed their faith, using the words of the Nicene Creed, first written in the fourth century to settle vigorous debates in the Church about the person and being of Jesus Christ. This Creed provides continuity through the turmoil of the Reformation with the earliest days of the Church. The same Creed would have been recited at William the Conqueror's coronation in 1066 and continues to be recited every Sunday at the celebration of Holy Communion in Westminster Abbey and throughout the Churches.

Now the service was moving inexorably towards the climax of the Coronation itself. This progress began with a beautiful and ancient hymn *Come Holy Ghost, our souls inspire* used when people are ordained and set apart for ministry in the Church as deacons, priests or bishops. It is an invocation, a calling on the Holy Spirit, a prayer that God will offer the sevenfold gifts of the Spirit to the person for whom the petition is made. This is a reference to a passage from Isaiah, where the prophet foretells that 'a shoot shall come out from the stock of Jesse, and a branch shall grow out of his roots. The spirit of the Lord shall rest on him, the spirit of wisdom and understanding, the spirit of counsel and might, the spirit of knowledge and the fear of the Lord. His delight shall be in the fear of the Lord.' This passage is often read as part of a Christmas carol service, so it is well known that Christians have always understood these prophetic words as applying ultimately to the coming of Jesus Christ, the fulfilment of the expectations of the people of Israel that a Messiah would be raised up, an anointed one. Jesus early in his ministry claims that this promise is fulfilled in himself. The invocation of these gifts of the Spirit on those to be ordained recognizes that in their ministry they represent Jesus Christ himself. This hymn is a preparation for the anointing with holy oil that in a sacramental way bestows the gifts.

As those who are being ordained are anointed, so the sovereign is anointed with holy oil. This makes the act of anointing very like an act of consecration, a setting apart for royal and priestly service, as if the monarch were an intermediary between God and the people. As Jesus Christ was anointed priest, prophet and king, so is the sovereign set apart for authoritative ministry under God, for the leadership of service. Following the hymn, the Archbishop prayed for the Queen to receive the sevenfold gifts of the Spirit, expressed in traditional language as gifts of wisdom and government, of counsel and ghostly strength, of knowledge and true godliness and of holy fear.

Now the high point arrived as the choir sang George Frederick Handel's anthem *Zadok the Priest*. 'Zadok the Priest and Nathan the Prophet anointed Solomon King. And all the people rejoiced, and said: "God save The King! Long live The King! May The King live for ever! Amen. Hallelujah!"'

The Queen moved from the chair on the south side of the Sacrarium, was disrobed of the crimson train and dressed in a simple white overgarment, and seated on the Coronation Chair, King Edward's Chair, set in the centre of the Sacrarium, under a canopy, facing the high altar. This part of the entire coronation ceremony alone was not televised, as being too personal and sacred to the Queen herself. The Archbishop anointed her with holy oil, in the sign of the cross on the hands, on the breast and on the crown of the head. He then prayed:

And as Solomon was anointed king
by Zadok the priest and Nathan the prophet,
so be thou anointed, blessed, and consecrated Queen
over the Peoples, whom the Lord thy God
hath given thee to rule and govern,
In the name of the Father, and of the Son, and of the Holy Ghost.
Amen.

Then the Queen knelt at a prayer desk (known as a 'faldstool') in front of the Coronation Chair, and the Archbishop prayed:

Our Lord Jesus Christ,

the Son of God,

who by his Father was anointed with the Oil of gladness

above his fellows,

by his holy Anointing pour down upon your Head and Heart

the blessing of the Holy Ghost,

and prosper the work of your Hands:

that by the assistance of his heavenly grace

you may govern and preserve

the Peoples committed to your charge

in wealth, peace, and godliness;

and after a long and glorious course

of ruling a temporal kingdom

wisely, justly, and religiously,

you may at last be made partaker of an eternal kingdom,

through the same Jesus Christ our Lord. Amen.

Then the Queen was clothed in vestments of cloth of gold, very like the dalmatic and stole worn by a deacon and a bishop and the cope worn by priests and bishops. This investiture has real significance, in that the Queen was seen to be given authority as a spiritual and religious leader. The Queen's authority as Supreme Governor of the Church of England is not purely temporal or worldly but spiritual and religious as well.

To this spiritual authority were added symbols of temporal authority under God: the sword, bracelets, the orb, the ring on the fourth finger of the right hand like a bishop's ring, the sceptre and the rod.

Finally the moment came of coronation itself, with the Queen still sitting before the high altar in King Edward's Chair. The Archbishop lowered the crown onto the anointed head of the Queen, praying:

> O God the Crown of the faithful:
> Bless we beseech thee this Crown,
> and so sanctify thy servant ELIZABETH
> upon whose head this day thou dost place it
> for a sign of royal majesty,
> that she may be filled by thine abundant grace
> with all princely virtues:
> through the King eternal Jesus Christ our Lord. Amen.

After this Blessing, the Queen moved from the Sacrarium to the centre of the coronation Theatre and, still accompanied by the Bishop of Durham and the Bishop of Bath and Wells who by long tradition act as supporters to the Sovereign, ascended the Throne set up high in the centre of the Lantern. The Archbishop prayed again for her, this time that the Queen's throne might be secure.

There followed one of the most precious moments, when the Duke of Edinburgh did homage to Her Majesty, using words that Prince Charles was to use years later at his investiture as Prince of Wales at Caernarfon Castle in 1969.

> I, Philip, Duke of Edinburgh
> do become your liege man of life and limb,
> and of earthly worship;
> and faith and truth will I bear unto you,
> to live and die, against all manner of folks.
> So help me God.

The archbishops and other national leaders did homage in the same way.

Meanwhile, the choir sang anthems concluding with the beautiful solemn prayer set to music by Samuel Sebastian Wesley:

Thou wilt keep him in perfect peace,

whose mind is stayed on thee.

The darkness is no darkness with thee, but the night is as clear

as day:

the darkness and the light to thee are both alike.

God is light,

and in him is no darkness at all.

O let my soul live,

and it shall praise thee.

For thine is the kingdom, the power and the glory,

for evermore.

Thou wilt keep him in perfect peace,

whose mind is stayed on thee.

Following a hymn, *All people that on earth do dwell*, in a new and glorious arrangement by Ralph Vaughan Williams, the service of Holy Communion was resumed, with the offering of the gifts of bread and wine, and a special prayer for the Duke of Edinburgh, in the rite of the Book of Common Prayer. The Queen and the Duke alone, in addition to the Archbishop of Canterbury as celebrant, received Holy Communion. Following the Blessing at the end of the celebration, the choir sang a solemn hymn of praise to almighty God *Te Deum*, *We praise thee O God, we acknowledge thee to be the Lord*, while the Queen accompanied by the Archbishop, various lay officers and the Mistress of the Robes withdrew to the Chapel of St Edward the Confessor behind the high altar, to be disrobed of the special royal and priestly garments with which she had been invested.

Then, dressed in a train of purple velvet, wearing the Imperial State Crown and carrying the orb and sceptre, the Queen left St Edward's Shrine and the Abbey church while the choir and congregation sang the National Anthem.

It is worth stressing and repeating that the essential stages of the service, although to some degree reorganized and sometimes reworded, have remained the same throughout the history of coronations in Westminster Abbey, where every monarch except two has been crowned since the medieval period began with the coronation of William the Conqueror. The two exceptions were Edward V, murdered as a boy with his brother the Duke of York in the Tower of London during the Wars of the Roses, and Edward VIII, who abdicated in 1936 before his coronation. With those exceptions, every reigning monarch has followed the same order of service. First they have been recognized and acclaimed. Next they have sworn oaths, been anointed with holy oil and crowned. Then they have been blessed by the Archbishop and received Holy Communion, according to the liturgy in use at the time.

Sometimes all this was done with considerable difficulty and against uncertain times. Changes were sometimes made in the liturgy at the last minute; often it was under-rehearsed and chaotic to a degree. Sometimes the monarch found the existing liturgical use strange and unwelcome. That was certainly true for Edward VI, the Protestant following his father Henry VIII, who, although he had broken with Rome, nevertheless retained the Catholic mass. His half-sisters, the Catholic Mary I and the Anglican Elizabeth I, were also crowned using a form which they would later change. Elizabeth in particular found it difficult. She moved away to a chapel during Catholic ceremonies of which she knew many of her subjects disapproved and that she would change: the Elevation of the Host and Chalice.

Sometimes, the monarch in question was considerably out of sorts with the religion of his country and it with him. When the Prince Regent who had been crowned as George IV eventually died in 1830, *The Times* newspaper reported of him: 'Never was there a human being less respected than this late king.' His coronation had been one of the most lavish ever, in accordance with his own tastes, but it is impossible to speak of that king's religious sentiments. Even so, the elements were all there, including the coronation oath, which had meant so much to his father George III, the anointing, the coronation itself of course, and the celebration of Holy Communion.

The words over the monarch in the coronation service, and the invocation of God's strength and grace at every stage in the service, point to the central reality of monarchy as understood in England and the United Kingdom in the tradition over the centuries, though not always observed in reality: commitment to a life not of self-glorification and self-gratification but of duty and service. Servant leadership is the key note throughout the coronation and it is a defining commitment which underlies the role the Queen has exemplified throughout the course of her reign.

There are strong antecedents for this understanding in the Jewish and Christian traditions, to be found in the Old Testament and the New Testament, in the example of priests, prophets and kings in the Old Testament and above all in our Lord Jesus Christ in the New

Testament. Associated with this pattern of servant leadership are clear notions of the virtues and values that should underpin our personal lives and our communal life, as peoples and nations. In the next chapter, I shall explore these concepts as understood in the Christian tradition that has shaped our society, not only in the United Kingdom and the Commonwealth but wherever English is spoken and the influence of the British people has been felt throughout the world.

Of the fruits of the Spirit, I have linked joy to this chapter in relation to the Coronation. Joy seems to me to be different from pleasure, which can have negative and selfish connotations, and even from happiness or contentment, which again can seem self-satisfied. I think of joy in the context of St Paul's instruction in his letter to the Philippians: 'Rejoice in the Lord always, and again I say, rejoice!' He goes on to tell us to worry about nothing but in everything to give thanks to the Lord. That develops a spirit of joy, even in the face of pain or difficulty – or the prospect of a lifetime of dutiful service. Duty can be joyful!

I conclude this chapter with the words of a prayer which we use daily in Westminster Abbey at the end of the quire offices, Matins and Evensong. It is an amalgamation of the prayer for the Queen's Majesty and that for the Royal Family in the 1662 Book of Common Prayer at the end of Morning and Evening Prayer:

> Almighty God, the fountain of all goodness, we humbly beseech thee to bless our most gracious Sovereign Lady Queen Elizabeth, Philip Duke of Edinburgh, Charles Prince of Wales and all the Royal Family. Endue them with thy Holy Spirit; enrich them with thy heavenly grace; prosper them with all happiness; and bring them to thine everlasting kingdom; through Jesus Christ our Lord. Amen.

2

Servant Leadership:
A biblical model

'The fruit of the Spirit is love, joy, peace, forbearance, kindness, generosity, faithfulness, gentleness and self-control' (Galatians 5: 22).

Generosity

What is leadership? What sort of person is a good leader? Is it someone who stands head and shoulders above everyone else, someone who looks good, or someone who can bend people to his or her point of view? Of course, different circumstances require different sorts of leader, whether it is on the playing field or the field of battle or the political arena or business or commerce or the arts. But, whatever the field, leaders can be expected to be dominant figures, to impose their will, to get their own way, by more or less subtle means.

But there is also a quite different idea of leadership, another model of a leader. Jesus Christ said to his disciples:

You know that among the Gentiles those whom they recognize as their rulers lord it over them, and their great ones are tyrants over them. But it is not so among you; but whoever wishes to become great among you must be your servant, and whoever wishes to be first among you must be slave of all. (Mark 10: 42-44; NRSV)

Of himself Jesus said that he 'came not to be served but to serve and to give his life as a ransom for many'.

This is quite a different model of leadership: leadership not as dominance but as service, not seeking to impose or to dictate, to make people follow, but to assist, to tend, to empower, to serve. This is leadership by example. I am calling it *servant leadership*. It is the kind of leadership Jesus Christ gave his disciples 2,000 years ago and gives his disciples still through the Church.

My contention is that it is to that manner of leadership that the Monarch is anointed, clothed and crowned. Moreover, Christian monarchy should – and does – set an example and provide a model for others in positions of leadership. In fact, it provides a model for everyone to follow. All of us exercise leadership in some way or another, if only in our daily lives, in our interactions with family and friends, with colleagues and neighbours, whether we lead organizations or not. We are called to be servant leaders. Indeed service itself is a form of leadership, in that it sets an example that others can be inspired to follow. The idea is not as familiar as it should be; nor is the example easy to follow. But I believe it is the kind of leadership the world needs and indeed that it is the only effective leadership that allows everyone to give of their best.

In this chapter, I trace the development of the idea of servant leadership through the Bible until it emerges in all its fullness and beauty in the life and death of our Lord. He sets us an example that we are all

called to follow. In this exploration, the idea of the leadership of monarchs is the starting point, because the anointing of the kings of Israel
is, as we know, explicitly referred to in the coronation service.

Servant leadership was not recognizably the model for the early kings
of Israel. The first rulers of Israel after Moses, when they returned to
the Promised Land from Egypt, were prophets and judges. Samuel, the
last of the judges to rule Israel, resisted strongly the people's insistence
that they wanted to be ruled by a king. He thought a king could never
be a good thing and would only present problems for their people.

The books of Samuel and the Kings in the Old Testament tell the
story. When Samuel was old, he appointed his sons judges over Israel.
But they took bribes and perverted justice. So the elders of Israel came
to Samuel at Ramah and asked him to appoint a king to govern them,
as other nations had a king. Samuel warned the people of Israel that a
king would try to dominate them, would take advantage of them.

Even so the elders of Israel insisted on their country being ruled by
a king. So Samuel set about the process of finding a man to be king.
The first he anointed was Saul, who was a great man, handsome and
head and shoulders above everyone else. He was successful at first.
But he turned away from the right path.

The choice of David as king is described as being most surprising. He is the youngest son and almost ignored; his father Jesse says:
'There remains yet the youngest but he is keeping the sheep.' He is
described as ruddy and handsome, with beautiful eyes. He eventually
establishes his rule and Jerusalem as his capital city. David defeats his
enemies and establishes a peaceful kingdom. And yet, he too behaves
in precisely the way Samuel has described. He sleeps with Bathsheba
who conceives a son and then, to cover up his sin, brings her husband

Uriah the Hittite home from battle so that Uriah can sleep with her and the child be seen as his. But Uriah refuses to leave the king's service, so David arranges for him to be put in danger in battle, where he loses his life. Later David repents and dies at peace with the Lord.

His son Solomon when he becomes king asks the Lord for the gift of wisdom. He proves to be a great and wise king and expands the kingdom. His wealth becomes legendary. He builds the first temple in Jerusalem. But, then the book of Kings tells us, he takes to himself seven hundred wives and three hundred concubines, and they turn his heart away from God. He abandons the worship of the Lord his God and builds high places to the worship of alien gods.

As the books of Samuel and the Kings tell the story, each of these kings was chosen by the Lord to rule his people, each of them had genuine virtues and partly obeyed the Lord's will, serving God and their people, but each of them in some way or another turned away from the Lord and behaved selfishly. In consequence, the kingdom suffered.

From the eighth century BC onwards, the Holy Land, already split into two separate kingdoms, Israel and Judah, suffered a series of assaults from neighbouring countries: the Assyrians, the Babylonians, the Persians, the Greeks, the Romans. The Roman Empire was still occupying the Holy Land in our Lord's time. The Assyrians overwhelmed the northern kingdom in the eighth century; the Babylonians the southern kingdom in the sixth century. The Babylonian exile, which lasted fifty years, was a crucial period of heart-searching and faith development for the leaders of God's people. The exiles were allowed back to the Holy Land under the rule of Cyrus the king of Persia and were able to restore worship in Jerusalem. The exile had been a devastating experience but had made the people of God think afresh.

We see the results of this fresh thinking in the book of the prophet Isaiah, conventionally understood to fall into two or three quite separate sections, the first dating from the eighth century and the second from the sixth towards the end of the exile. Early in Isaiah we read of the prophet's hope for a new dawn, a new age, when the nations of the world would look to Jerusalem, to Zion, the city of God, for the law and for the word of the Lord. Then they would 'beat their swords into ploughshares and their spears into pruning hooks: nation shall not lift up sword against nation, neither shall they learn war any more'. This new age would be heralded by

> a rod out of the stem of Jesse, and a Branch shall grow out of his roots: And the spirit of the Lord shall rest upon him, the spirit of wisdom and understanding, the spirit of counsel and might, the spirit of knowledge and the fear of the Lord; And he shall make him of quick understanding in the fear of the Lord. (Isaiah 11: 1-3; KJV)

The people of Israel were beginning to develop a belief that the Lord their God was in truth the God of the whole world, God for all nations, and a sense that they must make this known. So, they were beginning to develop a sense of themselves as a people who existed not for themselves alone but for the benefit of the nations, for the whole world, a sign of hope, a servant people. And the expectation grew of the coming of an individual who would focus the work of the Lord, a servant of God who would especially, perhaps uniquely, reflect the Lord's will and show the nations his way: someone specially chosen by God, his anointed one, his Messiah. This development in understanding is crucial and fascinating. Israel begins to conceive itself as existing not simply for itself, for its own prosperity, for its own relationship with the Lord God, but as having a duty beyond itself, to all nations, that they too might come to know and love the Lord the God of Israel. So we see the idea emerging of the nation itself as offering servant leadership for the benefit of other nations.

Later in Isaiah, during the time of the exile, this hope for a Messiah is refined, in the light of the suffering of the people of Israel, into an expectation of a Suffering Servant of God who will bear the grief of his people.

> He is despised and rejected by men; a man of sorrows, and acquainted with grief: and we hid as it were our faces from him; he was despised and we esteemed him not. Surely he hath borne our griefs and carried our sorrows: yet we did esteem him stricken, smitten of God and afflicted. But he was wounded for our transgressions, bruised for our iniquities: the chastisement of our peace was upon him; and with his stripes we are healed. All we like sheep have gone astray; we have turned every one to his own way; and the Lord has laid on him the iniquity of us all. (Isaiah 53: 3-6; KJV)

The servant of God and of his people must be willing to suffer, to accept privation, to bear the burden of leadership. We have now moved very far from the idea of leadership as dominance, as dictatorship, as bending subjects or citizens to the will of the leader. Leadership as service, bearing the burden, paying the price: this is the crucial background to the understanding of his role that it seems gradually dawned on

Jesus as he grew up and began his ministry. Jesus has no doubt when he speaks in the synagogue in Nazareth that the expectations of the Messiah, the anointed one, the Lord's and the people's suffering servant, have fallen on him.

> When he came to Nazareth, where he had been brought up, he went to the synagogue on the sabbath day, as was his custom. He stood up to read, and the scroll of the prophet Isaiah was given to him. He unrolled the scroll and found the place where it was written: 'The Spirit of the Lord is upon me, because he has anointed me to bring good news to the poor. He has sent me to proclaim release to the captives and recovery of sight to the blind, to let the oppressed go free, to proclaim the year of the Lord's favour.' And he rolled up the scroll, gave it back to the attendant, and sat down. The eyes of all in the synagogue were fixed on him. Then he began to say to them: 'Today this scripture has been fulfilled in your hearing.' (Luke 4: 16-21; NRSV)

The people of his own town rejected him but others began to follow him. The disciples of Jesus took some time to come to believe that he truly was the Messiah, the Christ. We see this dawning in the moment at Caesarea Philippi when Jesus asks his disciples who people say that he is (Matthew 16: 13ff). 'Some say John the Baptist, but others Elijah, and still others Jeremiah or one of the prophets.' In answer to Jesus' direct question 'But who do you say that I am?' Peter answers: 'You are the Messiah, the Son of the living God.' But the light only partially dawns. The disciples seem to see a promise of glory for God's people in Israel, of the triumph of his oppressed people and their impending freedom from the imperial Roman yoke. Jesus goes on to tell the disciples that he is to suffer and to be killed and on the third day be raised. They cannot take it in. Peter rebukes Jesus saying: 'God forbid it, Lord. This must never happen to you.' Jesus in his turn says to Peter: 'Get behind me, Satan!' But the other disciples too have failed to accept or understand that the Messiah must suffer and thus enter into his glory. James and John the sons of Zebedee, two of Jesus' earliest and closest disciples, on the way up to Jerusalem for the final conflict, ask Jesus to give them places of honour when he comes into his kingdom, one at his right hand and the other at his left. They fail to see that his kingdom is not of this world. Like most of the other disciples, when Jesus is arrested they desert him and flee. Peter himself swears allegiance to Jesus at the Last Supper and follows him to the house of the chief priest; there, challenged by the maid and other servants that he is a Galilean and must be one of his disciples, he denies with curses that he ever knew the man. He is not ready to join the Lord in his suffering, though when the cock crows and he remembers Jesus' foretelling of his denial, he repents and goes out and weeps bitterly.

Peter is eventually to discover that there is only one way of being a faithful disciple of Jesus Christ. He heard Jesus in his lifetime telling the rich young man to sell everything he had and give it to the poor, then to come and follow him. He himself heard the strong and challenging words of Jesus:

Do not think that I have come to bring peace to the earth; I have not come to bring peace but a sword. For I have come to set a man against his father, and a daughter against her mother, and a daughter-in-law against her mother-in-law; and one's foes will be members of one's own household. Whoever loves father or mother more than me is not worthy of me; and whoever loves son or daughter more than me is not worthy of me; and whoever does not take up the cross and follow me is not worthy of me. Those who find their life will lose it, and those who lose their life for my sake will find it. (Matthew 10: 34ff; NRSV)

I love the *Quo vadis* legend, which tells of Peter funking it again just as he had at the trial of Jesus, walking away from persecution in the city of Rome and meeting Jesus walking into the city. Peter is said to have asked Jesus, Quo vadis? Where are you going? Jesus answered that he was going into the city to be crucified again for Peter. In the end St Peter died a martyr's death. Rather than give up his loyalty to Christ, the suffering servant, he shared in his suffering. In Rome in the mid-60s, under the Emperor Nero, Peter was crucified, hanging upside down. Most of the apostles died in the persecutions of Jews and Christians under the emperor Nero, just as Christians were to die under the persecutions of various emperors through the first three centuries of the Church. Rather than being defeated by the persecution, the Church grew in strength. The blood of the martyrs was truly the seed of the Church.

St Paul died in Rome at the same time as St Peter. As a Roman citizen, he died by the sword. St Peter and St Paul are honoured together as the twin apostles and martyrs of the Eternal City. In several of his letters Paul wrote of sufferings on behalf of the Gospel of Jesus Christ and of his willingness to die for the sake of the Gospel. Writing to the Colossians, St Paul said: 'I am now rejoicing in my sufferings for your sake, and in my flesh I am completing what is lacking in Christ's afflictions for the sake of his body, that is the church' (Colossians 1: 24; NRSV).

This brings us close to the very heart of the Gospel, the good news in Jesus Christ. Let me repeat the words of Jesus I quoted earlier: '[W]hoever does not take up the cross and follow me is not worthy of me. Those who find their life will lose it, and those who lose their life for my sake will find it.' If we are to take seriously the challenge of our Lord to take up the cross and follow him, we must be prepared not only to suffer, but also to offer whatever is suffered in union with the suffering of Christ for the benefit of the Church and the world. This is the mysterious truth at the heart of the universe: that if we seek to grasp life, we shall lose it; but if we are willing to give up everything, to offer our lives in loving service, in virtuous and godly living, after the example of the saints, we shall find life, together with happiness and peace.

'Virtuous and godly living' is a quotation from the Book of Common Prayer Collect for All Saints' Day, when we pray that we may follow the example of the saints in virtuous and godly living. In the Introduction I spoke of Christian values as the values we should be living by. There is a great deal of use of the word *values* in our own day. One of the values people identify is freedom. That was certainly one of the values that inspired the French revolution: freedom, equality, brotherhood. We shall be thinking later about the value of freedom for others, freedom from slavery. We could also think of freedom from sin, opening for us the way to the perfect freedom which is to be found in the service of God. But it seems to me that to prioritize freedom for ourselves, as commonly understood, is precisely to go in the wrong direction, to be placing our own selfish needs and desires above everything else. St Paul said:

You were called to freedom, brothers and sisters, only do not use your freedom as an opportunity for self-indulgence, but through love become slaves to one another. For the whole law is summed up in a single commandment, You shall love your neighbour as yourself. (Galatians 5:13; NRSV)

Ours seems to be a selfish age, when people put themselves and their own interests ahead of everything else. Some politicians want to legislate to make us less selfish in practice, while others see self-interest as a powerful motivating force for development and growth. Commentators reflect when and how this attitude developed of me-first and the devil take the hindmost. Some look back on a golden age, the war-time spirit, or the 1950s, when attitudes were different. Some commentators would charge the 1980s with promoting the pursuit of personal success, indeed of excess, above all other considerations. The 1960s might be a better candidate with the wish of the hip generation to overthrow all convention, to cry freedom and make up new rules for living from day to day. But there was no golden age. Nor can governments be blamed. The ultimate culprit I would suggest is the age-old problem, the root or original sin, of putting ourselves first, of doing what pleases us at the time and caring nothing for the consequences. The ancient myth of Adam and Eve, true in its way for all time, tells us about human nature all we need to know.

Without the grace of God, we cannot live generously, giving of ourselves in loving service. Just as Jesus was anointed with the Holy Spirit at his baptism, so must we be anointed if our lives are to be committed to service. Our human nature, too often weak and wilful, can be transformed into the likeness of Christ by the grace of the Holy Spirit.

St Paul in his letter to the Galatians calls them, and us, to live by the Spirit and not to gratify the desires of the flesh. 'The fruit of the Spirit is love, joy, peace, forbearance, kindness, generosity, faithfulness, gentleness and self-control' (Galatians 5: 22; NRSV).

As the coronation church, and the place of burial and memorialization of so many kings and queens and other leaders of our nation with influence throughout the world, Westminster Abbey is peculiarly placed to give public witness to these values. Not only is the Abbey visited every year by at least a million visitors, for whom our aim is that they should become truly pilgrims, but there are also many thousands of people each week who attend acts of worship in the Abbey.

In addition to the daily and weekly round of worship, which is a strong basis for the life of the Abbey, are numbers of special services for particular occasions. These special services generally commemorate particular anniversaries or events of significance. Some are wreath-layings at the Grave of the Unknown Warrior or one of the other 3,300 graves or memorials, perhaps attended by a few people. Others are major services attended by a full Abbey of 2,000 people, perhaps attended by the Queen and the Duke of Edinburgh or another member of the Royal family, sometimes televised live by the BBC and in the case of the most significant events, other television channels. All these occasions give the Abbey the opportunity of witnessing to what is of fundamental importance in the Christian life, the fruits of the Spirit as described by St Paul: love, joy, peace, forbearance, kindness, generosity, faithfulness, gentleness and self-control.

We have seen the notion of leadership developing through the Old and New Testament from one of dominance to one of service, after the model of Christ, truly unselfish service that is willing not only to put others first but to suffer for others. We are called to live like Christ and insofar as we are leaders to be servant leaders. Through God working in us, through the gifts of the Spirit, that is possible. Then we shall demonstrate in our lives those characteristics of love, joy, peace, forbearance, kindness, generosity, faithfulness, gentleness and self-control.

The chapters of this book are headed by those words and one particular characteristic is identified in relation to the main theme of the chapter. This chapter's fruit of the Spirit is generosity. It is only when we think generously of the needs of others and put them before our own that we can be true servant leaders. God's love for us is not sparing or niggardly but generous, full, running over. So must be our response.

I hope it is true that the services I am describing in this book have given powerful witness to the particular characteristic, or fruit of the Spirit, identified with them. Each of these services reaches beyond itself and its influence continues reverberating, just as the Abbey itself has borne witness through a thousand years to the love of God fully revealed in our Lord Jesus Christ, whose example of servant leadership we are called to follow.

I was moved to hear public testimony to what I have been talking about here perhaps from an unexpected context, nevertheless one that reveals how deeply the idea of servant leadership has penetrated our way of thinking. During a BBC television documentary on Sandhurst, the British Army's officer training college, the Commandant said: 'I'm often asked, Is there one golden rule for leadership? As officers, you are serving your soldiers. Some day you may have to lead men into battle. This is an extraordinary thing to do. You are their servants, and you do this by leading them. . . . If you don't do that you haven't got it.'

J Armitage Robinson was the first Dean of Westminster to be appointed in the twentieth century. He wrote a beautiful prayer for the Abbey, which speaks of its ancient history and contemporary relevance. I hope you might wish to make it your own prayer for the Abbey.

O Everlasting God, with whom a thousand years are but as one day, and in whose name are treasured here the memorials of many generations: Grant to those who labour in this place such measures of thy grace and wisdom, that they may neglect no portion of their manifold inheritance, but so guard and use it to thy glory and the enlargement of thy Church, that the consecration of all human powers may set forward thy purpose of gathering up into one all things in Christ; through whom to thee be glory, now and evermore. Amen

3

Abolition of the Slave Trade bicentenary

'The fruit of the Spirit is love, joy, peace, forbearance, kindness, generosity, faithfulness, gentleness and self-control' (Galatians 5: 22).

Gentleness

The Abbey has a reputation for smooth calm efficiency. Everything generally goes like clockwork. Services start on time and run as planned. So it seems. But not always. One of my first really important services had an incident that made my heart beat faster. The best idea when things go wrong is to carry on as though what is happening is what was intended. That was not possible this time. I shall come to that soon.

Becoming part of the life of Westminster Abbey has been an extraordinary experience for me. I have always loved history, although I recognize great gaps in my knowledge. But at the Abbey it feels as though the currents of English history are flowing through the Abbey itself. Aspects of history of which I had only been vaguely aware suddenly come into focus and become fascinating. I had never supposed that I would wish to read a book on the life of Edward I. But there he is, buried near the shrine of St Edward the Confessor – so his life has become interesting. When I am at my seat near the high altar, just opposite me is a fine image of him, painted by an East Anglian artist in 1307, the year of his death. But the more you learn, the more you know how much there is to learn.

Gradually in my first few months, I became aware that there are numbers of people, most of them unknown to me, who know a great deal about the Abbey, its history, its architecture, archaeology, music, monuments. Beyond them it began to dawn on me were millions – literally millions – for whom there is some perhaps small but important link with the Abbey in their lives. I stand at the Great West Door after Evensong or Sunday services greeting as many of the hundreds of people leaving as I can. Some of the people I greet have been looking forward to this moment for years. They are often quite overwhelmed. I remember in particular my first such meeting. An Australian woman, perhaps someone who had retired, with tears in her eyes, told me that she had always longed to come to Westminster Abbey. For fifty years, she had hoped that one day this dream would be fulfilled. Now it had, when she came to Evensong, and it had been a wonderful experience. I was moved myself.

The Abbey is served by an amazing team of people, staff and volunteers, strongly committed to its life. Some of them have given more or less their whole working lives. Like me, they are aware that every one of the million or two visitors the Abbey receives every year needs to be welcomed in the right way. The Rule of St Benedict, by which the Abbey lived for six hundred years, continues to be important for the life and approach we seek to cultivate. The chapter in the Rule about the reception of guests begins by saying: 'All guests who arrive should be received as if they were Christ.' That is a tall order when there are so many but we do our best.

I find it particularly important to create opportunities of welcoming people who might not normally think of coming to the Abbey, and to reach out to make connections. I am impressed by the vision of the Dean and Chapter in the 1990s that led to the placing of images of twentieth-century martyrs in the niches above the Great West Door empty since the west front was finished in 1745. The installation there of twentieth-century martyrs was almost the last move of the great restoration that cleaned and repaired the Abbey from the mid-1970s until about 1996. That process was made possible through the fundraising of a committee chaired by the Duke of Edinburgh. Among those twentieth-century martyrs are Christians from every continent who died in that century as a result of their faith, representatives of a tragically great number of witnesses with their blood.

Each of the martyrs commemorated there offers us an opportunity to reach out to a part of the wider community. On the 40th anniversary of the assassination of Dr Martin Luther King Jr., we held a special service attended by many hundreds of people for whom his particular vision had been a liberation, and we sponsored with the US Embassy a conference, mostly for young black and Muslim people, aimed at helping them catch something of Martin Luther King's vision of peaceful but determined resistance and the dignity and worth of every human being made and loved by God. I hoped they would apply that vision to the experience of young people in our country in our own time. It was a good day that will continue to bear fruit. So much of the life of the Abbey enables us to touch one part of other people's lives; we hope others will carry it forward on the journey.

In a similar way, we observed the 40th anniversary of the assassination of Janani Luwum, the Ugandan archbishop. His killing had been ordered by that country's dictator, President Idi Amin, whose vicious rule he had opposed. It was wonderful to see the nave of the Abbey full of people with Ugandan connections at a Sunday evening service. Archbishop John Sentamu of York was himself born in Uganda and fled under Amin's rule. That evening he helped many hundreds of people with strong personal and family links in Uganda commemorate and celebrate Janani Luwum, the great martyr.

Those two commemorations reminded us of the cruelty and oppression suffered by so many. Before I arrived as Dean, plans were already afoot for a much more significant recognition of the horror of slavery, an ancient cruelty still wretchedly with us, and of steps towards its abolition. In 1807, William Wilberforce, a Member of Parliament and a committed Christian, working with many others in Parliament and elsewhere, had after many years achieved a milestone in the struggle against the slave trade. On 27 March 2007, we held a special service in the Abbey to commemorate the bicentenary of the passing into law in the United Kingdom and the British Empire of the Abolition of the Slave Trade Act.

The Abbey was the right place for the service. Wilberforce is buried in the Abbey's north transept and commemorated with a remarkable statue in the north quire aisle. Many other abolitionists are buried or commemorated in the Abbey. Each has his own remarkable story. One of them is particularly inspiring. Zachary Macaulay voluntarily travelled in a ship transporting slaves across the Atlantic from Africa to the West Indies (the so-called 'Middle Passage'). He kept notes in Greek secretly, before returning to share the evidence he had collected with his colleagues in the Clapham Sect. His memorial tablet is in the nave. Some of Wilberforce's supporters are well known for other reasons. John Wesley wrote to William Wilberforce. It was his last letter. He spoke of Wilberforce's 'glorious enterprise opposing that execrable villainy which is the scandal of religion, of England and of human nature'. He, with his brother Charles, is commemorated in the south quire aisle of the Abbey.

When the time came for the bicentenary service, I had been Dean for less than four months and the service had been in the Abbey programme for many months before that. This would be my first great special service, attended by the Queen and the Duke of Edinburgh as well as the Prime Minister and other political leaders and by representatives of the countries of the Commonwealth, and televised live by the BBC. No pressure.

As Dean, I am the Ordinary of the Abbey. That means I have authority in the Abbey, rather like a bishop in a diocese, though most decisions are taken by the Dean and Chapter together. The Canons have their own significant areas of responsibility in the Abbey: for the finances and fabric; for hospitality, education and the visitor experience; for our relations with the Palace of Westminster and Whitehall; for our theological thinking and public debate. They also take a lively interest in services, some of which they themselves conduct and which in any case they attend. I have particular responsibility for the Abbey's worshipping life. It would of course be impossible to exercise this responsibility alone. There are teams whose main role is to plan and prepare services, especially the Minor Canons and their colleagues. Others play key parts: among them the musicians, the vergers and the honorary stewards.

For any special service, there are external partners who generally have approached us themselves to propose the service. To promote and commemorate the bicentenary of the Abolition of the Slave Trade Act was an initiative of Churches Together in England and their commemorative organization *set all free*. The year was well marked with books, a feature film about William Wilberforce, television programmes, public lectures and exhibitions. Schools played their part. As a result of all these initiatives, not many people in the United Kingdom, or in large parts of the world, in 2007 were unaware of the bicentenary. People also recognized that, even though the transatlantic slave trade was effectively abolished and slavery has long been outlawed in most of the developed world, slavery continues in our own day as human trafficking, bonded and forced labour, slavery by descent and child labour.

I was determined that the Abbey congregation for the service would be inclusive and broadly representative of the churches of the United Kingdom. I was particularly keen that those churches with large numbers of people whose families had historically been disfigured by the horror of slavery would be well represented. So it was. Among the 2,000 people in the Abbey were many descendants of slaves alongside descendants of the abolitionists and representatives of the churches and other faith communities concerned at the contemporary impact of slavery. Before the Queen and the Duke arrived there was a procession to the Sacrarium of representatives of a great variety of churches and other Christian organizations. I was pleased to welcome Janet Scott of the Religious Society of Friends, the Quakers, whom I had met in my previous post at ecumenical discussions about Religious Education. The African and Caribbean Evangelical Alliance was represented. So was Holy Trinity Clapham, where William Wilberforce worshipped with other members of the influential Clapham Sect.

To help establish the right atmosphere before the service the Adventist Vocal Ensemble sang traditional African-American spirituals, and the Freedom 200 Chamber Orchestra played music by Le Chevalier de Saint-George, the eighteenth-century Afro-French composer.

George Alagiah, who was presenting the BBC broadcast of the service and would provide the commentary, interviewed me a day or two beforehand. We sat in the Jerusalem Chamber in the Deanery. He asked me about my expectations of the service. I told him I was concerned that with two rather different ideas coexisting each should have its own clear expression. It would not be very easy. The first idea was one of remembering the remarkable achievement of a small group of people who had worked over many years to abolish the transatlantic slave trade. William Wilberforce was pre-eminent among them in the public memory, but there were others, including, among a number of slaves who had managed to escape their confinement, Olaudah Equiano, who had later been baptized at St Margaret's Church Westminster. The second idea had two parts: to remember the suffering of those who had been enslaved and also to recognize that slavery continues in our own day. I hoped that the symbolic means we had devised for respecting these two elements would bring the service to a powerful conclusion: the Queen would lay flowers at William Wilberforce's memorial in the north quire aisle; then she would lay flowers at the Innocent Victims' memorial near the Abbey's west gate. These actions would, I hoped, speak louder than words. As I spoke to George Alagiah, one idea that did not occur to me was that I should also be concerned about the fact that there had been no government apology for our national involvement in historic slavery. I am not in favour of centuries-late retrospective apologies but am strongly in favour of acts of penitence. I felt sure that our powerful act of repentance in the service would express all that was needed.

The service fell into three parts, as I said in my welcome and bidding: 'We have come to *remember* the commitment and courage of the abolitionists, *reflect* in penitence on the destructive power of evil, and *respond* by committing ourselves to a world in which no one is enslaved.'

Remembering began with words written by Olaudah Equiano about his own personal experience:

I was soon put down under the decks, and there I received such a salutation in my nostrils as I had never experienced in my life: so that with the loathsomeness of the stench and crying together, I became so sick and low that I was not able to eat, nor had I the least desire to taste anything. I now wished for the last friend, death, to relieve me.

The Archbishop of York and I then received and offered at the high altar a copy of Olaudah's book *Interesting Narrative* and of the Act of Parliament of 1807 and we heard an extract from Wilberforce's own words in the House of Commons on 12 May 1789.

The Archbishop of Canterbury in his address quoted Jean-Jacques Rousseau's slogan 'Human beings are born free, yet everywhere they are in chains' and spoke of 'the Spirit that creates a community in which each takes responsibility for all as they become "members of one another"'.

We are not born free. But we are born for freedom. That is why, in this service, and in the act of repentance and restoration last Saturday, Christians of British descent invited others to join them and to speak to them some of the necessary words of judgement and of mercy. Is the Spirit contemporary and alive for us? If so, we shall indeed have the courage to face the legacies of slavery – the literal degrading slavery of the millions who, then and now, are the victims of the greed of others, and the spiritual slavery of those who oppress and abuse, and so wreck their own humanity as well as that of others. We shall have the courage to turn to each other and ask how, together, we are to make each other more free and more human. May that Spirit be upon us and in us in our struggles.

To drive the point home, before the confession, we heard then some details of the slave trade itself and also of the continuing existence of forms of slavery:

> During the four centuries of the Transatlantic Slave Trade, at least eleven million Africans were enslaved and transported. As many as two in ten perished on the ships which carried the Africans to the Americas. The life expectancy of an enslaved African on a plantation was seven years. Today, one hundred and forty million people in sub-Saharan Africa live on less than one dollar a day. More than twelve million people are in slavery worldwide. More than one million children are trafficked. Millions are affected by the global racism which has its origin in the Transatlantic Slave Trade.

This led to an act of repentance in a specially written confession, which began with the reminder that 'all have sinned and fall short of the glory of God'. We began the confession:

> Most merciful God,
> I confess to you,

before the whole company of heaven,

and to you my sisters and brothers,

that I have sinned in thought, word, and deed,

in my action and in my silence,

through prejudice or ignorance

or my own deliberate fault.

As we meet together before you, gracious Father,

we look at the past and we lament.

We look at the present, and we pray:

forgive us our sins,

renew our fellowship in your Spirit,

and raise us to new life in Christ. Amen.

During the words of the confession, I began to hear a disturbance, someone shouting, but I was standing at the high altar facing away from the congregation and could do nothing other than continue leading the confession. I then turned to pronounce the absolution:

May the God who in his grace seeks out and restores those who are lost, pardon and deliver you from all your sins, strengthen you in all goodness, and lead you home to eternal life in him.

What I saw was a shock, and yet there was nothing I could do other than stay calm and carry on, allowing the matter to unfold. I went to sit down. Causing the disturbance was a man standing a few feet from the Queen, directly between her and the Prime Minister. He was shouting a protest that the Government had not apologized. He called on everyone of African descent in the congregation to leave the Abbey with him. Not one of them moved. The police protection officers were by now standing between the Queen and the protester, and several Abbey staff and volunteers were moving in too. Eventually the protester was ushered out, but he resisted the route to the nearest exit and insisted on walking through the quire and the length of the nave. Gradually the Abbey fell quiet.

A black pastor leaving the church later told me that in his church the protester would have been lifted off his feet and removed rapidly. An American in the congregation told me afterwards that he wondered whether the President's security detail would not have solved the problem in a far more radical fashion. The Archbishop of Canterbury said afterwards that it had been like a second sermon. Later the police asked us whether we wished to press charges and, despite our rejecting the proposal and insisting that the incident was closed, the protester was kept in police custody overnight. There was full media coverage on radio and television and in newspapers the next day, with large and shocking pictures. But there were no follow-up stories and little public reaction to the news.

As I waited those few moments that were like an age I remember my greatest fear to be that the BBC would carry out their warning during the planning stages, that if the service was too long they would abandon us and switch to the 1 o'clock news. We had designed the service to end a couple of minutes to the hour. But I thought of the symbolic acts that came at the end of the service. The loss of those vital few minutes would leave the television audience with no sense of the powerful symbolic climax. I need not have worried. George Alagiah resisted his best news instincts, as the cameras roamed around various interesting aspects of the Abbey ceiling and only when the problem was almost over briefly focused on the departing protester. And the BBC 1 o'clock news started a few minutes late that day.

Naturally there were enquiries as to how the protester had found his way through the police vetting of the congregation and the elaborate security searches. It seems that he was accredited to a newspaper, which of course had no idea of his intention. It is unclear to me whether *he* had any idea at the beginning of the service, though it certainly seemed ironic that both the head of state and the head of government were expressing repentance precisely at the point when they were accused of not having apologized. The Church of England had in fact apologized, as the Archbishop had said in his address, and I hope that the service expressed genuine repentance (a different matter from an apology). We certainly intended to promote reconciliation.

The service continued with a most remarkable anthem by Grayston Ives, commissioned specially for the service, including quotations from the Psalms, Acts, Ephesians, Colossians and John Newton. Since the anthem began with a quotation from the psalms 'Out of the deep have I called unto thee O Lord' and ended with a quotation from *Amazing Grace* 'and grace will lead me home', it took up the pain of which the protester was speaking and placed everything in God's hands.

> OUT of the deep have I called unto thee, O Lord: Lord, hear my voice.
> O let thine ears consider well: the voice of my complaint.
> Consider my complaint: for I am brought very low.
> The sorrows of death compassed me: and the overflowings of ungodliness made me afraid. The pains of hell came about me: the snares of death overtook me.

Hear my crying, O God.

For strangers are risen up against me: and tyrants which have not God before their eyes seek after my soul. Save me, O God: save me from all them that persecute me: for they are too mighty for me. For the waters are come in, even unto my soul.

I stick fast in the deep mire, where no ground is: I am come into deep waters, so that the floods run over me. I am weary of crying, my throat is dry: my sight faileth me for waiting so long upon my God. Take me out of the mire, that I sink not: O let me be delivered from them that hate me, and out of the deep waters.

Out of the deep have I called unto thee, O Lord: Lord, hear my voice.

I saw a light from heaven, above the brightness of the sun, shining round about me; 'bright shining as the sun'.

For the Lord God is a light and defence: the Lord will give grace and worship.

'God's grace has brought me safe thus far.'

For by grace are we saved through faith: it is the gift of God.

Every one of us is given grace: it is the gift of God.

Let the peace of God rule in our hearts, singing with grace in our hearts to the Lord, 'and grace will lead me home'.

The exchange of Peace that followed was very special.

The final section *Respond* included a testimony from someone who had been trafficked as a child, and a Prayer of Commitment:

GRACIOUS and liberating God:
lift us beyond the burdens of pain and guilt,
build our memories into life-giving resolutions,

give us the vision of a new creation,

strengthen us to act for justice and human dignity

and set all free. Amen.

After the choir had sung words of Olaudah Equiano, quoting the prophet Micah, 'To look for the hand of God; become better and wiser, and learn to do justly, to love mercy, and to walk humbly before God', the Queen laid flowers, in honour of all abolitionists, at the statue of William Wilberforce in the north quire aisle and then, in honour of all who suffered and those who suffer still from the effects of slavery, at the Innocent Victims' memorial outside the west front of the Abbey. It all ended in peace and respect.

For me, it had been a remarkable service, and one which left me feeling proud of the institution I had joined and of all our staff and volunteers both for their confidence in handling a crisis and for the planning of a beautiful and significant service.

I have chosen particular fruits of the Spirit, as listed by St Paul in his letter to the Galatians, for each of the special services that I am discussing here. My view is that we each as Christians should be examining ourselves as to how we display the sevenfold fruits of the Spirit in our daily lives and also that unostentatiously in public ministry we might well think of ways of celebrating these gifts in public and holding them up as an example. I hope and pray that this ambition informs our approach at the Abbey to the high-profile special services that are part of the Abbey's ministry and mission.

I realize that reflecting on the fruit of gentleness might evoke for some the image of 'gentle Jesus meek and mild', which seems not to take into account the times when Jesus is angry or stern and, to a degree, uncompromising. I cannot see Jesus as gentlemanly, in the sense of polished and superficially courteous. But 'gentle' is a description St Paul uses of Jesus, and we must take it seriously. St Paul, whose reputation surely is not one of gentleness, says to the Corinthians: 'I, myself, Paul, appeal to you by the meekness and gentleness of Christ – I who am humble when face to face with you, but bold toward you when I am away!' (I Corinthians 10: 1; NRSV). I like the self-knowledge and touch of humour.

We are asked to demonstrate gentleness ourselves, by the grace of the Holy Spirit, and to witness to it in public. I hope that both the service I have been describing itself and also the way we coped with the protest upheld that ambition.

You might like to reflect on the continuing existence of slavery and pray for all those involved using the words of a prayer led in the service by Bishop Nathan Hovhannisian, Primate of the Armenian Church of Great Britain:

WE pray for those who endure modern forms of slavery – those who are trafficked, who are condemned to bonded labour, for children whose labour is exploited, and those who today are treated as commodities or cargo. We pray for agencies and individuals working to relieve their plight.

Lord in your mercy:

Hear our prayer.

4

The Queen and Duke's diamond wedding

'The fruit of the Spirit is love, joy, peace, forbearance, kindness, generosity, faithfulness, gentleness and self-control' (Galatians 5: 22).

Faithfulness

There is a charming legend that the first Abbey church was consecrated by St Peter the Apostle during the reign of Sebert, king of the West Saxons, who died in 616, while St Mellitus, consecrated in 604, was bishop of London. The apostle, unidentified at first, is supposed to have asked Edric a fisherman to ferry him across the Thames from the Lambeth side to Thorney Island, the site of the Abbey. The fisherman was asked to wait. As he waited he saw light shining from the newly built abbey church and heard sounds of chanting. Then the stranger emerged and asked to be rowed back across the river. The following morning, Bishop Mellitus found the oil of consecration dripping from the consecration crosses on the walls of the church. In the thirteenth century when it was most probably originated, this legend may not have seemed so charming to the authorities of the diocese of London or to those who felt they had some prior claim to the fish in the river Thames which the Abbot insisted were his. I like it, even though there is no evidence for it at all.

The Abbey's archives contain a vast number of documents from the Middle Ages. There is a tenth century document under the hand of King Egbert in which he grants land on and near Thorney Island to his relation, Dunstan, who is the bishop of London but about to become archbishop of Canterbury. The date is 960. Dunstan had been abbot of Glastonbury in Somerset and used his wealth and influence to establish or re-establish monasteries throughout the land. One of those would become known as the West Minster, no doubt to be distinguished from St Paul's Cathedral, the East Minster in the ancient city of London. So, the first Abbey we know of for sure dates from 960. There are no remains from that building. To the north of the current building, two bodies buried in the tenth or early eleventh century were uncovered by a recent *Time Team* programme for Channel 4 television. The bones were left undisturbed and decently covered again with earth.

That tenth century church was not to remain for long. In 1042 Edward became king of England, when he won the crown that was rightfully his from the Danish occupiers. Later ages would call him St Edward the Confessor. He had been in exile in Normandy, his mother's land, and had sworn an oath that he would make a pilgrimage to Rome when he won his crown. When King Edward found he was too busy and preoccupied in his new kingdom, the Pope dispensed him from the oath, on condition that he build a church dedicated to St Peter.

Edward began in 1045 to rebuild St Peter's, the Westminster Abbey church, and decided to establish his royal palace at Westminster too, away from the noise and smells of London. The Palace of Westminster has not been a royal *residence* since Henry VIII moved to a new palace at Whitehall. The Palace of Westminster is the Houses of Parliament, rebuilt after a devastating fire in 1834. But it remains a royal *palace*.

So at Westminster Church and State are yoked together. I find that a powerful statement about the national life of England, our understanding of ourselves. These neighbours buttress each other. Of course much of the time they challenge each other too.

Edward the Confessor's church was consecrated on 28 December 1065. It was almost as large as the nave and quire of the present Abbey church and in the Norman style that would become so familiar in England after the conquest. At that time, it must have been by far the greatest building in the kingdom and awe-inspiring. The *Abbaye aux Hommes* in Normandy is the burial place of William Duke of Normandy – William the Conqueror – who was building at about the same time as Edward was building his abbey church. Standing at the west end of that Norman nave in Caen, I began to get the feel of Edward's church. You see an almost endless vista of magnificent round arches and huge pillars with simple vaulting: such a confident and powerful statement.

Edward died on 5 January 1066 and was buried the following day, on the day of Harold's coronation, in front of the high altar. Some parts of the abbey buildings remain from his day: the Undercroft, the Pyx chamber and the dark cloister. He was canonized in 1161, as St Edward the Confessor, and buried in a more prominent position in his church on 13 October 1163.

By the thirteenth century, Edward is little regarded. But Henry III, king since 1216, remembers. He names his son after the saint;

he will be known as Edward I. In the 1240s, Henry begins to rebuild the church. The gothic style is now popular, with thinner, graceful piers, pointed arches and elaborate vaulting. His church challenges the prowess of the kings of France as builders. Henry can only go so far. The quire with the east end of the present Abbey church is consecrated on the feast of the Translation of St Edward, 13 October 1269. Henry III dies in 1272 and is buried near the shrine of the saint. His son Edward I has little time for building churches; he succeeds in conquering the Welsh but only hammering the Scots, and commits his energies as a builder to a chain of magnificent castles.

The next king to continue building the Abbey is Richard II. He comes to the throne as a boy and his reign ends bitterly. But he is pious. The magnificent Wilton diptych shows that he has a great devotion to two English kings who have become saints: St Edward the Confessor and St Edmund the Martyr. In his reign the process begins of progressively replacing the nave of Edward's church. Despite the style changes a hundred years bring, the nave is built in the style of Henry's church, so there is a beautiful continuity from east to west of the church. The work halts frequently over the decades. It is only in the reign of Henry VIII that the nave reaches its present extent and the western towers reach to the height of the roof. John Islip is Abbot from 1500 to 1532 and crowns the work, with an unbearable irony, only a few years before the monastery is dissolved. By then Islip has already rebuilt, at royal expense, the Lady Chapel at the east end of the church, which then becomes the burial place of Henry VII and his queen Elizabeth of York. The western towers, as we know them now, are much later, designed by Nicholas Hawksmoor, successor of

Sir Christopher Wren as surveyor of the fabric, and date from 1745 during the reign of George II.

There is a great deal more to be said about the buildings, but not here and now. I must give some account of what has happened in them. From the beginning, in 960 or earlier, the monks of the Abbey live under the Rule of St Benedict. That continues until the dissolution of the monastery by Thomas Cromwell under Henry VIII in 1540. The Abbey as the historic place of coronations and the burial place of his parents is too precious for the king to allow its destruction, the fate of so many monasteries. The king's alternative solution is to make them cathedrals with their own dioceses fresh minted for the purpose. For ten years, the abbey becomes a cathedral, the seat of a bishop, with a new diocese, carved out of the diocese of London. That can never have been comfortable, and in 1550 the Abbey's diocese is reintegrated with the diocese of London.

The sixteenth century is a hard time for the Church in England, and especially in the years of greatest turmoil between the 1530s and 1560. The Abbey's possessions, its land and property, are successively seized and restored. When in 1550 the Abbey ceases to be a cathedral, thirteen of its ancient manors in Paddington and Westbourne are ripped from the Abbey's grasp and transferred to the diocese of London. It must have caused quite a fuss. An old expression is still current today: they robbed Peter to pay Paul.

On 7 September 1556 Mary I re-founds the abbey, which is then dissolved again after the accession of Elizabeth I on 10 July 1559. On 21 May 1560, Elizabeth re-establishes the Abbey as the Collegiate Church of St Peter in Westminster, a Royal Peculiar. That means the Abbey is not part of the diocese of London or the province of Canterbury

so not answerable to the Bishop of London or the Archbishop of
Canterbury. The governing body is the Dean and Chapter, consisting
of four Canons, under the immediate authority of the Monarch as
Visitor. Thus it remains.

Throughout the years since 1560 and until today, the daily worship
of almighty God forms the foundation of the life of what is still famil-
iarly called the Abbey. There has been only one exceptional period:
the eleven years of the interregnum from the beheading of Charles I
in 1649, sometimes known as the Commonwealth, when horses were
stalled in the Abbey. For the rest of those 450 years, the worship has
been the daily offices of Morning and Evening Prayer and since the
twentieth century also the daily celebration of the Holy Eucharist.

But special services and events add character and profile. They
allow the Abbey, from its peculiar position as a place of religion, to
pay public witness to Christian virtues and values. The Abbey is a sign
of faith at the heart of national life. Coronations symbolize vividly
what that means. Royal weddings in their own way give public witness to Christian belief, in the doctrine of marriage.

There was a beautiful service to celebrate marriage in 2007. That
year the Abbey took part in the diamond wedding celebrations of the
Queen and the Duke of Edinburgh. The date was Monday 19 November, one day before the diamond wedding day itself. The Queen,
accompanied by the Duke, arrived to a fanfare and to the sight of
a full church. The congregation included the members of the Royal
Family and other relations of the Queen and Duke and many members of foreign royal families, the collegiate body of Westminster
Abbey, including the Queen's Scholars of Westminster School, who
were represented at the wedding in 1947. There were also couples

from across the country who had been married on the same day as the Queen and Duke, 20 November 1947. The Prime Minister was there and other political representatives with the Queen's representatives in each county, the Lord Lieutenants.

I was keen to ensure that the presence of church leaders from England, Scotland, Wales and Northern Ireland would allow people from every part of the United Kingdom to identify with the occasion. Representatives of the Jewish, Muslim, Hindu, Sikh, Buddhist, Jain, Zoroastrian and Baha'i faith communities were also there (as they are at many special services). An important part of the Abbey's mission, as I understand it, is to give access to other denominations and faiths at the heart of national life.

Some of the more colourful attendants on significant national occasions like this are the two corps of Her Majesty's Body Guards, the Gentlemen-at-Arms and the Yeomen of the Guard. Both Body Guards were founded in 1485, to give protection to the future king Henry VII during the Battle of Bosworth Field against the forces of Richard III. The Yeomen of the Guard are to be clearly distinguished from the so-called Beefeaters, the Yeomen of the Tower of London, though they are dressed alike in Tudor uniforms. They have a lively association with the Abbey. The year 2009 was the 500th anniversary of the death of Henry VII so they joined us for a service in the king's place of burial, the Lady Chapel at the Abbey, wearing full dress uniform, with the officers of the order and former officers, in the presence of the Queen and the Duke of Edinburgh.

At the diamond wedding five men who had sung as boys at the 1947 wedding were among the Abbey serving team, formed from the Brotherhood of St Edward, all of whom were at one time Abbey choristers.

Earlier in the year, the Dean and Chapter and the Abbey Old Choristers' Association had invited all the former choirboys from the service
to a reunion. Almost all of them came, some from overseas. I asked
them what, looking back over the intervening sixty years, they felt
they had gained most from their time as choristers. They all had a
continuing love of music, in which some of them had made their profession. Several mentioned the value of the self-discipline they had
developed at the Choir School, fitting in so many different demands.
Above all they had gained confidence through the pressure of public
performance at an early age. That had never left them.

The diamond wedding service spoke unostentatiously of the value
of faithfulness in marriage – not only to the congregation assembled
in the Abbey but for many times as many people through the medium
of live television. That is an important witness, since although the
divorce rate in the United Kingdom is currently going down, that is
only because the level of marriages is itself at its lowest since national
records began in the nineteenth century. In 2009, there were fewer
than a third as many marriages as in 1972.

But on 19 November 2007, the tone of the service was of thanksgiving and joy. Quite frequently, at silver weddings or ruby, golden
or diamond weddings, couples renew their marriage vows or make
some other personal statement of their commitment to each other.
It has always seemed to me rather an awkward thing to ask people to
do. And in the case of the Queen and the Duke, whose lives have been
so much in the public eye, it would have been redundant as well as
possibly embarrassing. In the event, we agreed that the Archbishop of
Canterbury, Dr Rowan Williams, would stand before them and offer
a special prayer that he had written himself.

That would be one element in the service. For the rest, as for any special service, we started with – almost – a blank sheet. 'Almost' because there are various well-established patterns and conventions for any service in the Abbey. Of course, there will be hymns, biblical readings, an address, or possibly more than one, prayers, an anthem sung by the choir and almost always other music sung by the choir as well. Typically, a service starts with the choir singing a short piece of music, called an Introit, that in some way sets the scene or helps to create the mood for the service. Then a hymn of praise accompanies the entry procession to set our minds on the worship of almighty God, and I welcome the congregation and outline the purpose of the service in the Bidding, which might or might not conclude with a prayer, the Lord's Prayer or a moment of silence. Once everything is under way the order of the content depends on the nature of the event. Sometimes at some point I might receive flags and lay them up at the altar, later returning them, or be involved in a procession to the Grave of the Unknown Warrior or the Innocent Victims' memorial in the western courtyard. As Dean I pronounce the Blessing at the end of the service.

Services attended by the Queen or another member of the Royal Family have their own additional conventions. Usually I receive distinguished visitors at the Great West Door and then present members of the Chapter and the visiting preacher to them before they are led to their place by an honorary steward. The Queen, accompanied by the Duke of Edinburgh, always arrives last and leaves first. There is only one exception to that rule: the Queen arrives before the bride at a wedding. I receive the Queen at the west gate and then walk with her into the Abbey to present the Canons.

How to arrange the procession and where the choir should stand to sing the Introit requires a degree of discussion between the Minor Canon preparing the service and the Organist and Master of the Choristers. On this occasion, the Introit was a setting of some beautiful words from psalms 48 and 118, 'We wait for thy loving kindness O Lord, in the midst of thy temple', sung at the Queen and Duke's wedding in 1947 and composed for the occasion. The Australian composer, William McKie, was at the time in charge of the music at the Abbey – and would be again at the Queen's coronation six years later. The choir sang standing on the nave side of the great organ screen and facing west. The collegiate procession with banners filled the nave. The Queen and Duke waited near me for the music to stop and the procession to start. It felt a little like a traffic jam.

When I finally reached the high altar, in my Bidding I introduced the themes of thanksgiving and of prayer, including prayer for marriages generally:

> [L]et us pray for those preparing to give their troth either to other; for the newly married; for those who are bringing up children; for the upholding of these relationships of love in times of joy and sorrow; and that marriage might be hallowed to the praise of God's holy name.

Prince William of Wales read a lesson about God's love and our response. I have no idea whether he thought at the time that his own wedding in the Abbey would follow in just over three years. It was from St John's plea that we should 'love one another, because love is from God; everyone who loves is born of God and knows God.' It was right then to sing *Come down, O Love divine*, with the prayer, *Let holy charity mine outward vesture be and lowliness become mine inner clothing, true lowliness of heart, which takes the humbler part.*

In his address, the Archbishop of Canterbury spoke of Christian marriage as 'a living sign of what God thinks about human capacity and human dignity, that God is to be trusted to be faithful – and that God trusts us to echo that faithfulness.'

> Every marriage is a public event, but some couples have to live more than others in the full light of publicity. We can give special thanks for the very public character of the witness and the sign offered to us by the marriage of Queen Elizabeth and Prince Philip, and what it has meant to nation and Commonwealth over the decades.

The Archbishop developed the theme of what that meant, likening to marriage the relationship between Monarch and people: 'a relationship in which we see what levels of commitment are possible for someone upheld by a clear sense of God's calling and enabling'. He spoke of the Queen's 'unswerving service' to the nation and to the Commonwealth.

The anthem is often after the address, to allow the thoughts expressed in the pulpit to resonate for a little longer. It is therefore important for the anthem to reflect the theme of the service, as the chosen music always must. When we decide that the occasion is sufficiently special, and perhaps the available music is not quite right, we commission an anthem. On this occasion Richard Rodney Bennett composed an unaccompanied setting of words from I Corinthians 13, St Paul's great chapter in praise of the primacy of love.

There is a lovely story that before the then Princess Elizabeth's wedding, the Princess and Princess Margaret, with one of the bridesmaids, Lady Margaret Egerton, sang to William McKie a descant to the tune *Crimond,* a Scottish metrical version of Psalm 23 *The Lord's my shepherd.* It was sung at the wedding and has since become very well known and loved. Of course Crimond had to be sung at the diamond wedding service.

I decided it would be good to have something non-scriptural read, something that would express emotionally the joy and respect everyone would be feeling. I telephoned the Poet Laureate Andrew Motion to ask whether he had planned to write a poem for the diamond wedding. He said he had nothing planned but would think about it. He came back to me very quickly to say he would write a poem. When I saw it, I was thrilled. It had I thought to be read by a woman capable of adequate power and we approached Dame Judi Dench, who agreed immediately. The poem *Diamond Wedding* made brilliant use of images of the diamond. Here is an extract:

> The years stacked up and as their weight increased
> they pressed the stone of time to diamond,
> immortal-mortal in its brilliant strength,
> a jewel of earth where lightnings correspond.
>
> Now every facet holds a picture-glimpse:
> in some the family faces, and the chance
> for ordinary talk and what-comes-next;
> in others show of pomp and circumstance.
>
> And here today, the diamond proves itself
> as something of our own yet not our own –

a blaze of trust, the oneness made of two;

the ornament and lodestar of the crown.

The moment for the Archbishop to read his own prayer for the Queen and the Duke would naturally come towards the end of the service:

Almighty God, the God of promise and faithfulness, who has led you together through so many years, renew in your hearts today the promises you have made to one another, and the sharing of your hope and joy; may he make your lives a sign of his own faithful love; may he strengthen and inspire the service you offer to the whole community of this nation and Commonwealth; may his living Word continue to transform and guide you and all whom you love; and the blessing of God Almighty, the Father, the Son, and the Holy Spirit, be with you and remain with you always.

John Rutter's popular setting of the Aaronic blessing brought the service to a gentle, meditative end: 'The Lord bless you and keep you. The Lord make his face to shine upon you, and be gracious unto you: the Lord lift up the light of his countenance upon you, and give you peace.' And then I pronounced the Blessing, using a version that always seems to me best for great national and Commonwealth services:

God grant to the living grace,

to the departed rest,

to the Church, The Queen, the Commonwealth and all mankind,

peace and concord,

and to us sinners life everlasting,

and the blessing of God Almighty: the Father, the Son and the Holy

Spirit, be among you and remain with you always.

The Queen and the Duke of Edinburgh viewed the Register, in which the registration of their marriage on 20 November 1947 was displayed. Finally the Queen, accompanied by the Duke, met those couples in the congregation who, like them, had been married on 20 November 1947.

The Abbey's stalwart Company of Ringers went on to ring the bells to a Peal of London (No 3) Surprise Royal comprising 5060 changes, a fitting climax to a glorious celebration.

I reflected afterwards on the nature of the celebration. At one level, this was a personal moment for the Queen and the Duke and for their family, a moment like that observed no doubt by all those celebrating 60 years of married life. If it had just been that, though, there would have been no reason why the service could not have taken place in a private chapel in Windsor Castle or Buckingham Palace. Such a service would no doubt have been more intimate, more personal, more relaxing than a great televised service in Westminster Abbey. But it is, as the Archbishop said in his address, the particular calling, the vocation, of the Queen, with other members of the royal family, to live their lives in a more public way than is the case for most of us. That very fact meant that we were able to celebrate not just the gift of this one marriage but the gift of marriage itself, and above all the gift of fidelity in marriage, the gift of faithfulness.

Faithfulness is one of the fruits of the Spirit, and the particular one of those fruits with which this chapter is identified. God's gifts, through his Holy Spirit, bear fruit in our own lives, the fruits of the Spirit. Faithfulness then is the result of God's gift in us. This suggests that we should not expect to be able to be very good at faithfulness in our own power, without God's help in our lives. The ultimate faithfulness is that of God for his creation, for his people. He is faithful to us and we can be faithful to God in response. If people try to live apart from this gift of God's faithfulness, it is no wonder that there is a failure to bear the fruit of faithfulness in so many lives. We must be consistent in praying that we and those we love can bear the fruit of faithfulness.

This prayer was read at the service by Commissioner Elizabeth Matear of the Salvation Army. You might like to use it in praying for the Queen and the Duke and adapt it to pray for members of your own family and friends who are married:

God of Abraham, God of Isaac, God of Jacob, bless these thy servants, Elizabeth and Philip, and sow the seed of eternal life in their hearts; that whatsoever in thy holy Word they shall profitably learn, they may in deed fulfil the same. Look, O Lord, mercifully upon them from heaven, and bless them. And as thou didst send thy blessing upon Abraham and Sarah, to their great comfort, so vouchsafe to send thy blessing upon these thy servants; that they obeying thy will, and alway being in safety under thy protection, may abide in thy love unto their lives' end; through Jesus Christ our Lord. Amen.

5

Commonwealth Day observance

'The fruit of the Spirit is love, joy, peace, forbearance, kindness, generosity, faithfulness, gentleness and self-control' (Galatians 5: 22).

Forbearance

When South Africa returned to the Commonwealth in 1994, a service of celebration was held in Westminster Abbey. The country's return to the membership of the Commonwealth was made possible by the end of apartheid and the establishment of government under President Nelson Mandela, happily now honoured with a statue in Parliament Square. In those days I was working in Lancashire as diocesan director of education and at Blackburn Cathedral but I still remember the images on television of Desmond Tutu, former Archbishop of Cape Town, dancing for joy outside the west front of the Abbey. In 2010, Desmond Tutu returned to the Abbey at the invitation of the Florence Nightingale Foundation to preach at the annual service in the Abbey that honours the memory of that remarkable nurse and celebrates the work of nurses in our own day. Two thousand nurses in the Abbey were thrilled to hear Desmond Tutu's encouragement and many lined up to meet him afterwards. The next day was Ascension Day and he preached for the Abbey's Sung Eucharist at 5, and a great congregation then was delighted to hear him. The influence of the Anglican Church leaders in the process of leading South Africa away from apartheid to majority rule comparatively peacefully was remarkable and encouraging.

Like many others of my generation, when I was young, I read Father (later Archbishop) Trevor Huddleston's *Naught for your comfort* and Alan Paton's *Cry, the beloved country* and found what I read there incredibly moving. So it was a privilege years later, in 2001, to be asked to visit South Africa and advise the Church of the Province of Southern Africa on its education policy. The Church, unwilling in the 1950s to implement apartheid restrictions in their many parish and mission schools, had handed them over to the government. I suggested that the government should be asked to hand them back, but had little hope that my advice would be received. Perhaps I did no more than reinforce something that was anyway likely to happen but I was thrilled when President Jacob Zuma came to the Abbey during a State Visit to Her Majesty The Queen and assured me that the government was indeed giving the Church back the schools that it had handed over more than fifty years earlier. I recognize that the Church might find it a difficult inheritance. Church schools do not become good schools overnight by virtue of the name at the gate. There is also the challenge of overcoming the ill effects of decades of underfunding and neglect.

South Africa's return to the Commonwealth in 1994 sealed an end to the terrible years of repression of 'non-whites' and mutual destruction that had been such a powerful source of international anxiety for decades. It was also an important moment in the history of the Commonwealth. The apartheid government in 1961 had broken ties with the Crown, declared South Africa a republic and left the Commonwealth. The fact that those ties were now restored was worthy of celebration. It was a happy time for the Abbey too. In the quire, many of the back-row stalls are labelled. Members of the collegiate body all have their proper places in the quire: the Abbey clergy; the senior staff; the High Steward and High Bailiff, offices of dignity now held by senior national figures; the senior staff of Westminster School. Three years ago we decided to add to the collegiate body the Administrator of Westminster Cathedral and the Superintendent Minister of Westminster Central Hall, our Roman Catholic and Methodist neighbours. So they have stalls too.

Then there are four more stalls with permanent labels: Canada, the Union (sic) of South Africa, Australia and New Zealand. These four senior members of the Commonwealth became self-governing dominions under the Crown a hundred or more years ago. For thirty-three years the South Africa stall plate had awaited the return of its significance. Also labelled is a seat simply saying High Commissioner, which has suspended beneath it the name of the country whose High Commissioner is to occupy the stall on any particular occasion. There was an important development in the Abbey's relationship with the Commonwealth in the 1970s during the time of Dean Edward Carpenter. He issued – and we have since continued to issue – an annual invitation from the Dean and Chapter to the High Commissioners of Commonwealth countries to attend Evensong on or near their country's national day, to bring with them some of the staff of the High

Commission and fellow nationals and to read the Second Lesson (which the Dean would normally read himself). The High Commissioners appreciate the invitation and honour it. Sometimes they bring large, sometimes smaller, numbers of people with them. A few years ago, I decided that we should advance the invitation to the predominantly Muslim countries rather than presuming that they would not wish to accept it. In practice, happily, most of them do. I remember the delight with which the representatives of Pakistan came for the first time and wanted large numbers of photographs after the service. Often they will also find a member of the staff of the High Commission who is a Christian to read the Second Lesson from the New Testament at Evensong.

This important relationship between the Abbey and the Commonwealth is reflected and strengthened in the annual service, attended by the Queen in her capacity as Head of the Commonwealth, accompanied by the Duke of Edinburgh, on Commonwealth Day, which is always the second Monday in March. The annual service has been held at the Abbey for many years though the tradition was created at St Martin in the Fields.

The service attracted a good deal of controversy especially in the 1980s from a group of Evangelical Anglicans on the grounds that it included as participants representatives of faiths other than Christianity. It is traditionally known therefore not as a service but as the Commonwealth Day Observance; although it has many elements of a service, it also contains elements of performance.

Commonwealth Day always falls in Lent. During that holy and penitential season, some of the exuberance of decoration in the Abbey is muted by hangings of unbleached linen which we call Lenten array.

Covering the nineteenth-century mosaic image of the Last Supper behind the high altar is Lenten array marked with the symbols of the passion of our Lord. In my first year at the Abbey, I found it incongruous that, at this service, the high altar was obscured from view by Commonwealth flags. The flags themselves I was pleased to see, with their bearers representing every country of the Commonwealth, but I was not persuaded that they should be paraded into position around the Sacrarium. There were other aspects of the planning that surprised me. The Abbey clergy were dressed in 'red and black', cassocks and gowns, rather than choir dress or surplices and copes, as is usual for special services. The other faith leaders represented their faith's perspective on the theme of the day not through prayer in their own tradition or even through a reading from a sacred book but through personal reflection on the teachings of their faith. Much of this I found strange but could understand how it had developed out of a spirit of defence of a principle under threat. It seemed to me that we could take some steps to dress and fashion the event as a service, introduce more clearly familiar elements of Christian worship, and allow the other faiths to represent more clearly their own tradition.

Our partner in planning the service is the Council of Commonwealth Societies, representing twenty-five different associations dedicated to the Commonwealth ideal, led by the Royal Commonwealth Society. In recent years there have been questions about the impact the service makes outside the Abbey with the broadcasters reluctant now to honour the significance of the Commonwealth itself and of this Commonwealth Day celebration. But for the 2,000 people, including school groups and people from all the Commonwealth countries, it is a great and worthwhile celebration.

In 2009, the theme *the commonwealth@60 serving a new generation* recalled the foundation of the post-imperial Commonwealth in 1949. But the intention of the celebration was not to look back but forward, to ensure that young people are committed to the Commonwealth ideals.

I believe in the value of the Commonwealth as the only international organization below the level of the United Nations that is not either regional like the European Union or based on wealth like the G7 or G20. The diversity of the nations is a genuine strength: large and small; rich and poor; ancient and modern; Christian and Muslim. I long for this to be better understood and valued. That is why I drew attention to this strength in my Bidding:

> The Commonwealth to which we all belong is enriched by the diversity which each nation brings to it. It is a community of nations which actively seeks to strengthen the bonds of understanding and where links of friendship can be forged, underpinned by the values we hold in common. For this reason the Commonwealth is dear to us at Westminster Abbey. This year's Commonwealth Day theme is concerned with the future, the new generation. The contribution of children and young people is a highlight of our celebration. Whilst they through word and music convey to us all the rich diversity of our community of nations, may each of us take a moment to consider how we might ourselves best serve the young people of the Commonwealth so that they can be nurtured and enabled to fulfil their God-given potential.

The Queen always records a Commonwealth Day message, which is printed in the order of service and heard pre-recorded by the Queen herself. She is herself the point of continuity for the Commonwealth: there from the beginning; genuinely giving active commitment and support.

This year the Commonwealth commemorates its foundation sixty years ago. The London Declaration of 1949 was the start of a new era in which our member countries committed themselves to work together, in partnership and as equals, towards a shared future. We can rightly celebrate the fact that the founding members' vision of the future has become a reality. The Commonwealth has evolved out of all recognition from its beginning. It has helped give birth to modern nations, and the eight original countries have become fifty-three. We are now home to nearly two billion people: a third of the world's population. Across continents and oceans, we have come to represent all the rich diversity of humankind. Yet despite its size and scale, the Commonwealth to me has been sustained during all this change by the continuity of our mutual values and goals. Our beliefs in freedom, democracy and human rights; development and prosperity mean as much today as they did more than half a century ago. The call that brought the Commonwealth together in 1949 remains the same today. Then we joined together in a collective spirit – built on lasting principles, wisdom, energy and creativity – to meet the great tasks of our times.

The theme of strength in diversity was amply demonstrated by the various organizations that contributed to the worship before and during the service. For example, we heard a traditional South African folk song originally sung by all-male work gangs, in a call and response style. Kiribati dancers offered a celebration of the island's staple diet, fish and coconut, and of the skills of the dance.

One element in the service was aimed at encouraging us not to give up in the fight for justice. A young Nigerian woman, Hafsat Abiola, spoke of the experience of living under military rule:

> Outraged by the poverty experienced by the majority of our people, we decided that we Nigerians must have a voice in the decisions that our government takes. So my parents and others started a movement for democracy and I joined it. We marched. We sang songs and we demanded change. Both my parents died for the cause. But, in the end, Nigerians brought an end to military rule and restored democracy. The task does not end there. I work now to teach our women that in a democracy, our votes give us power to end poverty, to create a just country, to contribute to making a better world. In my generation, let the Commonwealth help build that world where wealth is created and truly held in common.

She concluded by asking religious leaders their response to the question of whether one person can challenge the way a whole society lives. The Venerable Bogoda Seelawimala responded from the Buddhist tradition:

> Yes, certainly he can. Like many other great teachers, the Buddha himself challenged the way in which people were living. He questioned their habitual assumptions and attitudes, and specifically said that his teaching went 'against the stream', meaning that it went against the tendency of most people to run after selfish desires and sensual pleasures in the hope that they will bring

lasting happiness. In one of our books it says: 'Think not lightly of evil, saying, "It will not come to me." Drop by drop is the water pot filled; likewise, the fool, gathering it little by little, fills himself with evil' (Dhammapada 121). All of us can take responsibility for our own actions and strive to live a virtuous life.

Another faith representative, Mrs Fidel Meehan, responded from her own tradition:

To the individual striving for the betterment of the world, 'Abdu'l-Bahá, one of the Central Figures of the Bahá'í Faith, says: 'Trust in the favour of God. Look not at your own capacities, for the divine bestowal can transform a drop into an ocean; it can make a tiny seed a lofty tree. Verily divine bestowals are like the sea and we are like the fishes in that sea. The fishes must not look at themselves; they must behold the ocean which is vast and wonderful. Provision for the sustenance of all is in this ocean, therefore the divine bounties encompass all and love eternal shines upon all.' In such ways can the individual challenge the way society lives and works for the common good.

Through further such exchanges, through prayers and affirmations, everyone in the congregation was encouraged to make his or her own commitment to the ideals of the Commonwealth. After each such service, the team responsible for it at the Abbey holds a wash-up meeting with me to see what has gone well or badly and to discuss how next year's service might be improved. We sometimes receive helpful feedback from others involved in the service. One problem we recognized was how it might be possible to apply the wisdom of the different faiths equally effectively to a theme chosen for the annual celebration by the Commonwealth societies. I decided we should make some changes to the approach, aimed at reducing the element of variety performance and worthy wordiness and increasing the sense of an act of worship recognizable as Anglican but also inclusive of other faiths. This would fit appropriately with my understanding of the role of the Abbey as a place of clear Anglican faith and worship at the heart of the nation which also promotes mutual respect and understanding between the faiths and gives access for the other faiths represented in our society. Crucial to this change would be the question as to whether we could with integrity and without violence to our Christian understanding allow prayers from other faith traditions to be said in the Abbey. This is a sticking point for some Christians. I decided that it should not be a sticking point for us. There is only one God. I believe in God's full revelation through our Lord Jesus Christ. Even so, we see through a glass darkly. I can stand alongside someone praying to the one God in a different way from me and be strengthened by the experience. Fifty years ago, Roman Catholics would not pray with Anglicans. Now, thank God, I have prayed in the Shrine of St Edward as the Pope and the Archbishop of Canterbury knelt there side by side.

On 8 March 2010, the theme of the celebration was *Science, Technology and Society* and, along with the Queen and the Duke of Edinburgh, the Prince of Wales and the Duchess of Cornwall attended the service. In a change from previous years, the clergy wore blue copes and the altar was visible and the candles lit. The flag-bearers entered and left in procession but dispersed around the congregation, where in fact the flags were better seen. For the first time not just the Choristers but the Choir of Westminster Abbey sang for the service much loved and familiar music reflecting the scientific theme in terms of God's glorious creation: *And the glory of the Lord* from Handel's *Messiah* and *The heavens are telling* from Haydn's *Creation*.

On 14 March 2011, the theme was *Women, agents of change*. The information at the beginning of the order of service included several potent reminders of the importance of the theme:

> Around the Commonwealth – out of 54 heads of government, only three are women – over two thirds of people living on less than one US dollar a day are women . . . 24 million people are living with HIV and women account for more than half of all newly-infected adults. . .
>
> Around the world . . . gender-based violence causes more deaths and disabilities among women of child-bearing age than cancer, malaria, traffic accidents, and war combined . . . two thirds of the children denied school are girls . . . civilians account for more than 70% of casualties in conflicts and most of them women and children. . .

In my bidding I related the theme of the service to the Christian tradition and to the Abbey:

> Our celebration this year of women as agents of change has a particular resonance for those of us who honour Mary, by God's grace the Mother of the Lord Jesus. We honour too Queen Elizabeth I and many other women of our island story, buried or memorialised here in the Abbey, who have been agents of change for the better.

The Commonwealth has its Head, the Queen, but also a head of government with a key role, called the chairperson-in-office. For the first time in 2011 this was a woman, the Prime Minister of Trinidad and Tobago. She read St Luke's account of the annunciation and the Abbey choir sang Charles Villiers Stanford's setting of the Magnificat in G. The popular singer Annie Lennox gave an address, wearing a t-shirt that read *HIV Positive*.

The Queen mentioned in her message an important initiative of the Commonwealth:

> And also this year, the Commonwealth reflects on what more could be achieved if women were able to play an even larger role. For example, I am encouraged that last year the Commonwealth launched a global effort to train and support half a million more midwives worldwide.

Carol Ann Duffy, who succeeded Andrew Motion as Poet Laureate, read her own poem, which had been commissioned for the service *A Commonwealth Blessing for Girls*:

> Here are the gifts we wish and the wishes
> we gift to new girls born, Antigua to Zambia,
> breathed blessings at cradles, from Canada
> to Trinidad, sent out by song, poetry, prayer
> to Bangladesh, Gambia, Jamaica, Kiribati, Tuvalu,
> to fall as rain on good crops or fill a cup
> with water, a toast to each bright daughter-
> health; the soul-wealth learning brings;
> friendship's dancing rings in Cameroon, Guyana,

New Zealand, Pakistan; equality, a girl half
of the whole of the harmed world, healer; the joy of choice;
a boy-loud voice; her life a loved light in Britain,
India, Malaysia; lastly we wish she gives
back in return to us her blessings, her unique gifts.

Prayers were led by a Methodist and a Salvation Army Commissioner, by Rabbi Tony Bayfield, Dr Natubhai Shah of the Jain community, Malcolm Deboo, a Zoroastrian, and Dr Indarjit Singh, the Sikh leader whose contributions to *Thought for the Day* are well known to any listener to *Today* on BBC Radio 4. I wondered whether I would receive any complaints about this praying together from the different faiths. Not one letter of complaint or word of rebuke came my way.

Dr Shah's prayer was familiar, written by Satish Kumar, a member of the Jain community, and adopted in 1981 by the movement *Prayer for Peace*:

Lead me from death to Life, from falsehood to Truth.
Lead me from despair to Hope, from fear to Trust.
Lead me from hate to Love, from war to Peace.
Let Peace fill our heart, our world, our universe.

Dr Singh's prayer is also worth recording, quoting as he frequently does on the radio from the thoughts of the founder of Sikhism, Guru Nanak. I do not believe his prayer could be thought in any way offensive to Christians.

'It is to women, condemned by men as inferior, that we are born.
In women we seek companionship and life-long marriage;
how can we call inferior those that give birth to royalty

and are central to all our lives?'

These words of Guru Nanak on the lowly status of women still sum
up the plight of women in many parts of the world today:

O Lord give us the wisdom to heed the Guru's sentiments and resolve
to ensure that women everywhere have the opportunity to work
for what Sikhs call 'sarbar ka bhalla', or the well-being of all.

Before the Blessing, the Secretary-General led an act of affirmation to
the Commonwealth. Frankly I am inclined to find this a slightly wooden
exercise, wordy and worthy rather than thrilling and inspiring. On the
other hand, our commitment to common values is important:

We affirm that every person possesses unique worth and dignity.

We affirm our respect for nature, and that we will be stewards of
the earth by caring for every part of it, and for it as a whole.

We affirm our belief in justice for everyone, and peace between
peoples and nations.

In 2011, with our theme of 'Women as Agents of Change', we
affirm our collective belief that where women prosper, societies
prosper. In word and deed, we will continue to seek new ways to
show solidarity and to support women and girls practically and
meaningfully, in order to fulfil all our human potential.

The congregation replied:

We affirm our belief in the Commonwealth as a force for good in
the world, and pledge ourselves to its service, now and in the
future.

As always, the diverse congregation included school groups from
around the country. Pupils from Westminster School were there, who

have undertaken a role in the school as Commonwealth ambassadors. I am proud of the fact that our Abbey school has taken up the theme of the Commonwealth quite vigorously. This group met regularly through the year to develop their own thinking about the value of the Commonwealth, and also met some Commonwealth leaders, and conducted their own direct research on a visit to New Zealand. I arranged for the group to meet the High Commissioner for Lesotho, HRH Prince Seeiso, so that they could learn of the value of the Commonwealth for a small and poor country. What impressed them was the evidence he gave of the increased capacity his country had gained through contact with other Commonwealth countries to enable them as a representative of the poorest nations to play a useful part in some international negotiations.

The Commonwealth represents a great diversity of countries that nevertheless share a common history and common values. It also has a high correlation with the Anglican Communion. It must be important to the Abbey. The annual Commonwealth Day celebration is a fixed point in the Abbey's calendar.

The value we are considering in this chapter is forbearance or patience. St Paul writes about God's forbearance: 'Do you despise the riches of his kindness and forbearance and patience?' (Romans 2: 4). We are also called to bear one another's burdens: 'Bear one another's burdens and in this way you will fulfil the law of Christ' (Galatians 6: 2). Many years ago a slogan for the Anglican Communion was 'mutual responsibility and interdependence'. That ambition seems these days beyond our reach, but it is a worthwhile objective, both for the Anglican Communion and for the Commonwealth.

I commend this prayer to you, offered by the Reverend Tony Miles at the 2011 service:

> O God the ruler of all, bless Elizabeth our Queen, and all the nations of the Commonwealth and their leaders. Give wisdom and vision to those who govern the peoples of the world; and grant us peace and justice that men, women, and children of every community may live in mutual respect. This we ask through Jesus Christ our Lord. Amen.

6

Remembrance

'The fruit of the Spirit is love, joy, peace, forbearance, kindness, generosity, faithfulness, gentleness and self-control' (Galatians 5: 22).

Self-control

November is the month of remembrance both for the Church and for the nation. The feast of All Saints on 1 November reminds us of all the holy men and women who have carried out God's will on earth and now share in the joy of heaven. The commemoration of All Souls the next day enables us to remember all those we love and see no longer and to pray that they too may enjoy the glory of heaven. Armistice Day and Remembrance Sunday have in the last century become in the United Kingdom national days of commemoration, when we call to mind all those who have lost their lives in the terrible conflicts of the last century.

After the Second World War, Remembrance Sunday, following 11 November, replaced Armistice Day as the day of remembrance. Now we have both. In these recent years of war in Iraq and Afghanistan, the two minutes' silence on Armistice Day, 11 November, the day the armistice was signed that brought the First World War to an end

in 1918, has become almost universally observed, with people standing still and silent in shops and railway stations and in offices around
the country. It is little remarked that 11 November in the Church's
calendar of saints is the commemoration of St Martin of Tours, the
good soldier who gave half his cloak to a beggar. I find that a happy
concurrence.

At the Abbey, remembrance focuses around the Grave of the
Unknown Warrior, buried on 11 November 1920 near the west end
of the nave. The Grave is surrounded by poppies, the first flower to
raise its head from the mud of the devastated First World War battlefields, and so a symbol of new life and hope. The earth in which
the warrior is buried came from the battlefields and the ledger stone
is of Belgian black marble. It was David Railton, an army chaplain,
who wrote in 1920 to the Dean, Herbert Ryle, to propose the burial,
the first in the world of an unknown warrior. Railton believed there
should be a national focus for those whose loved ones were missing
presumed dead, buried, as so many, unidentified in a grave with the
inscription *a soldier known only to God*. Ryle was reluctant to accept
the idea. Perhaps he thought it would stir up unhappy memories two
years after the end of the war. Finally he put the idea to George V, who
also required some persuading that the proposal would be welcomed
by those most closely affected. When the moment came for select-
ing the unknown warrior, four unidentified bodies were brought
from different battlefield cemeteries in northern France to a chapel
in Saint-Pol-sur-Ternoise near Arras, where a blind-folded brigadier
general pointed at random to one. The body was placed in a plain coffin and brought across the channel on HMS Verdun and then to Victoria Station. It was taken on a gun carriage to Whitehall, where the

cenotaph designed by Sir Edwin Lutyens as a permanent memorial to the dead of the Great War was to be unveiled by the king. George V then attended the State Funeral of the Unknown Warrior in Westminster Abbey. A hundred holders of the Victoria Cross, awarded *For Valour*, for the most courageous action in the face of the enemy, lined the route. A hundred widows, who had lost not only their husbands but all their sons in the war, were in attendance. After the interment, servicemen kept watch while thousands of people filed past the Grave. Near the Grave now are hung David Railton's Union Flag, which was said to have been draped over the coffin, and also the ship's bell of HMS Verdun, and the US Congressional Medal of Honour awarded to the Unknown Warrior in 1921 and brought to the Abbey by General Pershing.

The Grave is a considerable focus of attention and has a powerful symbolic effect. On 10 December 2007 we held a service of remembrance and thanksgiving for the Second Battalion of The Rifles when they returned from a tour of duty in Afghanistan's Helmand province. Nine men had lost their lives and over thirty had been seriously injured. The Minor Canon responsible for drafting the service and I thought long and hard about how we could create a powerful moment of remembrance and thanksgiving in relation to those nine men. Actions are often more powerful than words. Their families would be present, so it was important that there should be a solemn moment for remembrance and commendation. This is what happened. The battalion's commanding officer laid a wreath at the Grave of the Unknown Warrior and then nine companions of the dead soldiers each carried a thick candle from the Grave right through the Abbey church to place them on the high altar. They then withdrew through the doors on either side into the Shrine of St Edward. I scarcely remember a more powerful ceremonial moment in the Abbey. I understand that, for those young men, it was an extraordinarily moving experience. I hope it was cathartic for all the relatives and friends of the dead and for those seriously injured too. As I greeted people leaving at the end of the service, it seemed to have been appreciated.

The Grave is an important focus on many occasions. Kings and Presidents and other heads of state making a State Visit to this country come to the Abbey after lunch on the first day to lay a wreath at the Grave of the Unknown Warrior. I offer a formal welcome on behalf of the Dean and Chapter standing at the Grave, the head of state lays a wreath and I lead prayers for peace and for our two countries. Then I take the head of state on a brief tour of the Abbey. The entourage follows.

Barack Obama, President of the United States of America, paid a State Visit starting on 24 May 2011. He and the First Lady came to the Abbey that afternoon. Once the formal ceremony was over and all the introductions had been made, including a warm greeting for every member of the choir, the Sub-Dean gave First Lady Michelle Obama a tour of the Abbey while I took the President. The conversations, as on this occasion, are often congenial and interesting. The President and First Lady signed the distinguished visitors' book, the President writing as follows: 'It is a great privilege to commemorate our common heritage, and common sacrifice.' He asked me to remind him of the spelling of *commemorate*. In fact, he had that right. He asked for the date as well. I reminded him it was 24 May but failed to mention the year. The media later made something of the fact that he had written the date as 24 May 2008, something I had failed to notice. A gaffe, they said. Nonsense; a simple mistake!

On occasions, heads of state making government visits join us at the Abbey too. Within a short space of time, I welcomed the President of Lebanon and the President of Israel, the latter arriving with an unplanned but irresistible surge of TV cameras broadcasting live into his country and preceding us all the way round the Abbey. Other memorable visitors have been the President of France, soon after his marriage to Carla Bruni-Sarkozy, and those of South Africa, Ghana and Mexico. The Emir of Qatar and his wife, Sheikha Mozah, visited the Abbey but, as Muslims, would not pray at the Grave. Instead they joined a small group in a short interfaith dialogue in the Jerusalem Chamber of the Deanery. It was a good moment.

The Grave is also the focus on remarkably different occasions. In 2010, we were asked by the chaplain at Pirbright, an initial training centre for soldiers destined for specialist service in the army as technicians or cooks or drivers or nurses, whether we would be willing to receive groups of young men and women at the end of their first five weeks in the army. The proposal was that they would come to the Grave of the Unknown Warrior for an introduction and a period of reflection and prayer and then have a tour of the Abbey. It would be part of a weekend in which they would undertake visits that would help them think about the army's code of values. After careful thought the Dean and Chapter agreed and now, once or twice a month, one, two or three squads of new soldiers in green combat dress assemble round the Grave. We believe the visits serve a useful purpose in initial training. I hope these recruits, some of whom will be facing danger very quickly, will above all remember that the Abbey honours them and prays for them, and that they will retain a little of the sense of the extraordinary history of which they are part.

There are many memorials to soldiers, sailors and airmen in the Abbey and its cloisters. Two memorials have been erected and dedicated in the south cloister during my time as Dean. One to all those who have died in active service of their country since the end of the Second World War was presented to the Dean and Chapter by HRH The Princess Royal. Another to the work of the Security Service (MI5), the Secret Intelligence Service (MI6) and the General Communications Headquarters (GCHQ) was presented by HM The Queen, accompanied by the Duke of Edinburgh, the Prime Minister, Foreign Secretary and Home Secretary, in the presence of 54 members of the three services. The event was held in high secrecy, but I regretted that there was little recognition of it in the media afterwards. It is a fine and worthy memorial, at the east end of the south cloister.

Other memorials and books of remembrance commemorate aspects of the work of the Army, the Royal Navy and the Royal Air Force. Groups of veterans come on a Saturday morning to turn the pages of the memorial books that line the north side of the nave. An upstairs chapel in the north ambulatory, dedicated to nurses, I rededicated in honour of Florence Nightingale in 2010, on the centenary of her death. There lies a book with the names of all the nurses who lost their lives in the Second World War. The book is offered at the high altar in the annual commemoration of Florence Nightingale on the second Wednesday in May.

In the Battle of Britain memorial chapel at the far east of the Lady Chapel is the book of remembrance of those who lost their lives in that battle, of whom Winston Churchill said: 'Never in the field of human conflict has so much been owed by so many to so few.' We remember, at the Battle of Britain memorial service in the Abbey, on the third Sunday in September. Before the service, some of the veterans join others at a wreath-laying at the grave of Lord Dowding in the chapel. They then join me for coffee in the Deanery before the service. It has been a privilege getting to know some of them and their close families. I am full of admiration for these old men, of tremendous character and determination as well as an abiding sense of humour, without which, I imagine, they could not possibly have sustained the fight. One of the oldest of them, Flt Lt William Walker, recited on one occasion to me in quick succession from memory three poems he had written – two of them very funny – in a gentle way.

Remembrance is a major theme at the Abbey. Every year a few days before Armistice Day, the Royal British Legion Field of Remembrance in St Margaret's Churchyard, to the north of the nave of the Abbey, is initiated with a small ceremony at 11 am including two minutes' silence and Last Post and Reveille. For many decades, Queen Elizabeth The Queen Mother would place her poppy of remembrance into a large cross of poppies. In the past decade, the duty has generally fallen to the Duke of Edinburgh. After the formal ceremony, there follows an hour-long tour of the sections of the Field, each attended by representatives of the regiment, squadron, fleet or unit concerned. The Duke then signs the visitors' book in St Margaret's Church.

Remembrance Sunday itself is of course the key annual focus of remembrance. We hold a special service that begins at 10.30 and is carefully timed to allow the two minutes' silence to take place at the Grave of the Unknown Warrior. The aim is for the Russian Contakion for the Departed to fall silent just in time for the chimes from the Bell Tower of the Palace of Westminster, leading up to the eleven strikes of Big Ben itself. All those involved who can affect the timing, especially the Master of the Choristers, who directs several minutes of music leading up to the precise moment, have detailed timings and digital watches attached to our service folders. Frankly, it is a little nerve-wracking, since we all feel the pressure to get the timing exactly right. It seems to work, though it feels a little harder when some guardsman who should perhaps have had an earlier night and a better breakfast keels over.

There was a little more pressure at a very special service that would have a high national profile. It was on 11 November 2009, when we held a service starting just before 11 am to commemorate the passing of the World War One generation. There had been extensive discussions with the Ministry of Defence about how exactly to mark the moment when the last of the long-lived veterans of the Great War finally died. At one time it had been suggested that the last to die should be given a state funeral. I understand none of the veterans was particularly keen on the idea. And we knew we should all have looked a little foolish if a hitherto unknown survivor had suddenly appeared too late. So, some kind of service was planned in theory, possibly starting at the Cenotaph in Whitehall, though in the end this was ruled out as impractical. Now the moment had come. The three remaining veterans of World War One living in the United Kingdom had died during the year: William Stone 108 in January, and Henry Allingham 113 and Harry Patch 111 in July. At the culmination of the service, the Queen would lay a wreath that had rested on the high altar and been borne to the Grave of the Unknown Warrior by two holders of the Victoria Cross, Trooper Mark Donaldson VC of the Australian Army 1st Battalion and Lance Corporal Johnson Beharry VC of the Princess of Wales's Royal Regiment. The service would start at the west end of the nave, with an introit and bidding and then the two minutes' silence at the Grave of the Unknown Warrior.

Split-second timing would be key to an effective beginning of the service. We had to arrive at a moment of silence thirty seconds before 11 o'clock, since Big Ben's chimes begin twenty-five seconds before the hour. Crashing the chimes would be unthinkable and even a few seconds' extra silence would seem unprofessional. Officials at Buckingham Palace worked closely with us. But the arrival of the royal car a couple of minutes either way could present problems. We worked out all the variables: what could be cut if the car was a little late; how to spin out the time if it was a little early. Of course, on other occasions none of this matters. When the Queen arrives the service starts. But this was different. Not today! In fact the car arrived about one minute before the due moment and the presentations moved slightly faster than we had expected. I had a little time to point out to the Queen the reason the Grave was covered in poppy leaves; they had been left by members of the public. Slowly I led the Queen to the appointed place. The choir sang the setting of Laurence Binyon's lines *They shall grow not old* by a former Abbey organist, Douglas Guest. I moved to the west side of the Grave to give the bidding. I still had a little too long and gave more emphasis to the words of the Bidding than was strictly necessary. Once I had brought it to a conclusion at exactly 10:59:30 I felt all would go as planned and could relax. The bidding ran:

Exactly ninety-one years ago, at the eleventh hour, on the eleventh day of the eleventh month, the guns fell silent. The Great War was over. Lives, friendships, families, societies, nations had been shattered. Everything had changed.

On this day two years later and at this hour, an Unknown Warrior, chosen at random to represent all those of these islands who had fought and died, accorded the highest honour of a state funeral, was buried here. His grave was to become the focus of our national remembrance and to have international significance.

Now that the last of his comrades in arms has gone to his eternal rest, we are here once more to remember. We remember, with grief, the gas and the mud, the barbed wire, the bombardment, the terror, the telegram; and, with gratitude, the courage and sacrifice. Never again, they said; the war to end all wars. With resolution we remember.

Two readings followed; the first by Anne Davidstone, the daughter of William Stone, was the ancient story in the book of Genesis of brothers at war:

CAIN said to his brother Abel, 'Let us go out to the field.' And when they were in the field, Cain rose up against his brother Abel, and killed him. Then the Lord said to Cain, 'Where is your brother Abel?' He said, 'I do not know; am I my brother's keeper?'

The answer to the question should of course be Yes, I am my brother's keeper. We are all responsible for each other. And we are all, as children of one heavenly father, brothers and sisters.

The second reading was given by the teenage son of an officer serving in Afghanistan and descendant of a naval officer in the First World War. This reading from the last book in the bible, the Revelation of St John the Divine, was full of hope:

THEN I saw a new heaven and a new earth; for the first heaven and the first earth had passed away, and the sea was no more. And I saw the holy city, the new Jerusalem, coming down out of heaven from God, prepared as a bride adorned for her husband. And I heard a loud voice from the throne saying, 'See, the home of God is among mortals. He will dwell with them; they will be his peoples, and God himself will be with them; he will wipe every tear from their eyes. Death will be no more; mourning and crying and pain will be no more, for the first things have passed away.' And the one who was seated on the throne said, 'See, I am making all things new.' Also he said, 'Write this, for these words are trustworthy and true.' Then he said to me, 'It is done! I am the Alpha and the Omega, the beginning and the end. To the thirsty I will give water as a gift from the spring of the water of life.'

After a hymn, the Archbishop of Canterbury, Dr Rowan Williams, gave an address. He began by recalling the devastation caused by the First World War not only to a whole generation of young men but also to national self-confidence:

The brilliant glow of the Edwardian autumn, about which so much has been written and imagined, gave way to the cruellest winter conceivable. An automatic belief in national righteousness, governmental wisdom, the trustworthiness of official communication and popular media alike – all these were shaken apparently beyond repair. The generation that discovered this had to find their way forward into the twentieth century with maps and landmarks damaged almost unrecognizably.

'Some features of the map survived.' He mentioned the army chaplain and poet, Geoffrey Studdert-Kennedy known as Woodbine Willie, and his commitment to 'the God who is discovered in the heart of your own endurance and pain'. And yet

perhaps what made the spreading effect of the war so lethal and corrosive, what helped the rising tide of scepticism and the sense of the absence of value and meaning throughout the century, was that the sort of question Studdert-Kennedy asked was rapidly forgotten. Too many religious people went back to a comfortable God. Too many people in general dusted off the clichés of the pre-war period – and too many simply reacted with anger and contempt against all of that. The sad standoff between despairing selfishness and superficiality on the one hand and inhuman new political philosophies on the other (communism and fascism) was fostered by a readiness to forget the hard lessons learned by those who'd been on the front line. In the darkest places, you discover you are real to yourself and one another. And if you're not called – mercifully – to such places, you will need disciplines of thinking and imagination to keep yourself real: to fight off easy answers, false gods, stifling systems. Prayer is one such discipline, essential and focal for people of faith; but there are others. We can still choose honesty or dishonesty. We can still choose what Chesterton called the 'easy speeches that comfort cruel men'; or we can choose to face how vulnerable we all are and how much we need to fight against our fear of one other if trust and hope and love are to prevail when all is done. The challenge is how we stay awake to how the world is – and to how it can yet be changed.

The Archbishop concluded:

The generation that has passed walked forward with vision and bravery and held together the bonds of our society, our continent, our Commonwealth through a terrible century. May we learn the lessons they learned; and God save us from learning them in the way they had to.

Jeremy Irons read a poem, *Last Post*, written by the Poet Laureate Carol Ann Duffy at the time of the death of Harry Patch. When I first read it, I found it both intensely simple and profoundly moving, based on the idea of a cine film run backwards. If only we could wind back the clock. So, often hindsight teaches us our errors. How rarely we learn.

IN all my dreams, before my helpless sight,
He plunges at me, guttering, choking, drowning.
If poetry could tell it backwards, true, begin
that moment shrapnel scythed you to the stinking mud. . .
but you get up, amazed, watch bled bad blood
run upwards from the slime into its wounds;
see lines and lines of British boys rewind
back to their trenches, kiss the photographs from home –
mothers, sweethearts, sisters, younger brothers
not entering the story now to die and die and die.
Dulce – No – *Decorum* – No – *Pro patria mori.*
You walk away.
You walk away; drop your gun (fixed bayonet)
like all your mates do too –
Harry, Tommy, Wilfred, Edward, Bert –
and light a cigarette.
There's coffee in the square,
warm French bread

and all those thousands dead

are shaking dried mud from their hair

and queuing up for home. Freshly alive,

a lad plays *Tipperary* to the crowd, released

from History; the glistening, healthy horses fit for heroes, kings.

You lean against a wall,

your several million lives still possible

and crammed with love, work, children, talent, English beer, good
    food.

You see the poet tuck away his pocket-book and smile.

If poetry could truly tell it backwards,

then it would.

At the Grave again, we heard the words of our Lord: 'Greater love has
no man than this, that a man lay down his life for his friends. You are
my friends if you do what I command you.' I introduced the wreath-
laying:

> This year has seen the passing of the three remaining veterans
> of World War One living in the United Kingdom: William Stone
> in January, and Henry Allingham and Harry Patch in July. Their
> names we honour. Now we remember and honour, by the laying
> of this Wreath, all those of their generation who, together with the
> Unknown Warrior, served during the First World War, those whose
> names we know, and those whose names are known to God alone.

While the band played Edward Elgar's Solemn Prelude *For the Fallen*,
the wreath was carried to the Grave and laid there by the Queen. The
bell of HMS Verdun was rung. The Chief of the Defence Staff, Sir Jock

Stirrup, said the words of Laurence Binyon earlier sung by the choir and all responded: 'We will remember them.' Last Post and Reveille were sounded. The choir then sang a hopeful setting of the final words of the eighth chapter of St Paul's epistle to the Romans, resplendent with Alleluias, specially commissioned by the Dean and Chapter from John Tavener:

> Who shall separate us from the love of Christ? Neither death, nor life, nor angels, nor principalities, nor powers, nor things present, nor things to come; nor height, nor depth, nor any other creature shall be able to separate us from the love of God, which is in Christ Jesus our Lord.

After a final prayer, celebrating the triumph over death of our Lord Jesus Christ, I gave the Blessing and we sang the National Anthem.

You might like to make that final prayer your own, as you reflect on the fruit of the Spirit, self-control, so fundamental for servant leadership, and the remarkable circumstances of so many people's lives that we recall during the season of remembrance:

> CHRIST our King, risen victorious over sin and death; shed your peaceful light on all mankind, and quicken this world with the brightness of your dawning. By your holy and glorious wounds, free us from all blindness and bitterness of heart, from disease of mind or body, from doubt or despair; grant to all your children your loving-kindness and newness of life in your name; and perfect in us the image of your glory; that we may join our praises with the praises of heaven, where you live and reign, with the Father and the Holy Spirit, one God, world without end. Amen.

7

The Papal Visit

'The fruit of the Spirit is love, joy, peace, forbearance, kindness, generosity, faithfulness, gentleness and self-control' (Galatians 5: 22).

Peace

At first I dismissed the speculation that Prime Minister Gordon Brown had invited Pope Benedict XVI to visit Great Britain. Then it began to look likely to happen and possibly even to be categorized as a State Visit. If so, it occurred to me, he should pay his respects at the Grave of the Unknown Warrior. I thought I would try to make sure he did. Some critics were still making an issue of the young Joseph Ratzinger having been a member of the Hitler Youth at the end of the Second World War, albeit briefly and unwillingly. So, all these decades after the world wars of the twentieth century, his coming to the Grave would still be a powerful symbol of peace and reconciliation.

I thought I might have an opportunity for a word about it with Archbishop Vincent Nichols. He was due to come to the Abbey in October 2009 for a first formal visit following his inauguration in May as Roman Catholic Archbishop of Westminster. In his previous ministry in Westminster and Birmingham, he had been at the Abbey many times. But his first visit as Archbishop of Westminster would be a significant occasion – with an interesting precedent, part of the long history of the post-Reformation Abbey's links with the Roman Catholic Church in England and Wales.

When it had been announced that George Basil Hume, the Abbot of Ampleforth, would become Archbishop of Westminster, following the death of Cardinal Heenan in 1975, Edward Carpenter, who had been a Canon of Westminster for many years but had quite recently taken office as Dean, visited the Benedictine monastery in Yorkshire where Basil Hume had spent much of his life. He wanted to establish friendly relations. What happened may well have exceeded his expectations. Following his episcopal ordination and installation as archbishop on 25 March 1976, Basil Hume came with the monks of Ampleforth down Victoria Street from Westminster Cathedral to Westminster Abbey to sing Vespers in the quire of the Abbey, much as it had been sung there by the monks of the Benedictine monastery from 960 for six hundred years. I know from one of the Ampleforth monks, himself later Abbot of Ampleforth, that it was a remarkable and wonderful experience.

That Vespers must have had added poignancy for the Roman Catholic Benedictine community on account of its strong links with the Abbey. The pope in 1607 had erected the English Benedictine Congregation in exile on a slender thread: the one monk still alive who had been part of the Benedictine monastery Mary I had revived at Westminster Abbey in 1556.

The Abbey had been dissolved as a monastery by Henry VIII in 1540 and had become first for ten years a cathedral with its own diocese and then been treated as a co-cathedral with St Paul's for the diocese of London. Mary I in 1553 brought England back to the Roman Catholic Church and, on 7 September 1556, only two years before her death, appointed John Feckenham, Dean of St Paul's, to be abbot of the revived monastery at Westminster. Elizabeth I after her accession on 17 November 1558 was keen to preserve the monastic community within her Church of England, Catholic and Reformed, and as a guarantee and condition invited Feckenham to accept the Archbishopric of Canterbury, vacant by the death on the same day as Mary I of Cardinal Reginald Pole. Feckenham refused and went to the Tower, spending the rest of his life in custody, though not always under close confinement. Elizabeth I finally decided that the monastery must be dissolved again on 10 July 1559 and the Queen in Council issued a charter establishing the Collegiate Church of the Blessed Peter in Westminster on 21 May 1560.

Some of the monks became prebendaries or minor canons of the collegiate church; no doubt some escaped into a life of private poverty; yet others escaped into exile while remaining loyal to their monastic vows. One of these last, Father Sigebert Buckley, the last surviving monk of Westminster – the slender thread I mentioned earlier – was given authority by the pope to clothe and profess on 21 November 1607 two novices, Robert Sadler and Edward Maihew, and thus to re-establish the English Benedictine Congregation. The Roman Catholic abbeys in England in our own day, among them Ampleforth, Downside, Douai and Quarr, see their origin as being from that papal act and look to Westminster Abbey as their monastic link with the pre-Reformation Church in these lands.

The link was renewed and strengthened when the archivist at Ampleforth approached me soon after my installation in 2006 with the suggestion that we might arrange an event at Westminster Abbey to commemorate the 400th anniversary. In November 2007, it was a pleasure to welcome to an afternoon conference in the Jerusalem Chamber most of the abbots of the English Benedictine Congregation and several of their colleagues. They heard a paper from Barbara Harvey, who has spent much of her long academic life among the Abbey archives. The abbots and their colleagues joined us for Evensong, followed by prayers in the Shrine of St Edward the Confessor and at the chapel of St Benedict.

The chapel of St Benedict, to the south of the Sacrarium, is dominated by the bust of the poet and satirist John Dryden and, being full of tombs and memorials, lacks an altar. One of the tombs in St Benedict's chapel is that of Simon Langham, the only Abbot of Westminster to become Archbishop of Canterbury and then a cardinal. He was also Treasurer and Chancellor of England. Since, as part of the long medieval battle for control of the Church in England between the Crown and the papacy, Edward III would not allow him to be a cardinal as well as archbishop, he moved to Avignon in the south of France, where the fourteenth-century papacy was based. The remuneration of his various church offices made him wealthy. His legacy to the Abbey helped his successor, Nicholas Lytlington, in the reign of Richard II to begin the process of replacing Edward the Confessor's Romanesque nave in the style of Henry III's Gothic church, a process not to be completed for two centuries. Basil Hume arranged with Edward Carpenter to have a quarter of an hour alone for prayer at the tomb of Cardinal Langham at the time of his receiving the red cardinal's hat. Sadly, his plane back from Rome was delayed and arrived too late in the

evening before a big service in Westminster Cathedral the following morning. So the moment passed.

Basil Hume's visit to the Abbey in 1976 following his inauguration
as Archbishop of Westminster established a pattern. The links continued to develop. In the year 2000, when Cormac Murphy O'Connor
followed him as archbishop, he too accepted an invitation from the
Dean, then Dr Wesley Carr, to attend Evensong, this time for an ecumenical formal welcome. The cardinal has been a real friend of the
Abbey, frequently attending services and other events at the Abbey.
Just before his retirement in 2009, he came for a private visit to the
Abbey with his auxiliary bishops, secretary and former secretary and
nun. I was delighted to give them a tour and to pray with them at
the joint tomb of the daughters of Henry VIII, the successive queens
Mary and Elizabeth, where the cardinal's representative had prayed
with the representative of the Archbishop of Canterbury at a special
evensong on 17 November 2008, the 450th anniversary of the death
of Mary and accession of Elizabeth.

Like my predecessors, hoping to continue strengthening the link
of friendship between the Abbey and the Roman Catholic Church in
these lands, I had invited Vincent Nichols to attend Evensong in the
Abbey during the Edwardtide festival in 2009. This was to be the joint
Evensong for the choirs of the Abbey and Cathedral which for some
years has been held around 13 October, the Feast of the Translation
of St Edward the Confessor, and attended by the priest administrator and chaplains of Westminster Cathedral. Vincent Nichols brought
with him in addition his auxiliary bishops and the cathedral canons.
The Archbishop of Canterbury had also accepted my invitation to
be present. I gave a formal welcome at the beginning of Evensong to

which Archbishop Nichols replied. At the end of Evensong, the two archbishops censed the Shrine of St Edward and prayed there. Then I hosted a congenial dinner in the Jerusalem Chamber, during which I heard briefly from Vincent Nichols about what might emerge for the papal visit. I recalled the lecture Pope Benedict had given on his visit to Paris at the Salle des Bernardins and offered the thought that he might use the visit to the Abbey as such an opportunity. I resolved anyway to write to the papal nuncio at Wimbledon with a formal invitation to the Pope to visit the Grave of the Unknown Warrior. It had not occurred to me that we might hold a big ecumenical service at the Abbey.

As detailed plans emerged, it became clear that the organizers hoped that a service at the Abbey would be the single ecumenical moment of the papal visit. It would take place after the Pope had addressed a joint assembly of members of the House of Commons and House of Lords in Westminster Hall. This was to be very different from the pastoral visit of Pope John Paul II in 1982. Although he had visited the Queen at Buckingham Palace, most of John Paul II's engagements were with the Roman Catholic community, with the exception of an ecumenical service with the Archbishop of Canterbury in Canterbury Cathedral. This would be the first papal visit to the Abbey in its thousand-year history. I was conscious of some irony: that, despite an intimate relationship between the Abbey and the papacy for 600 years, no pope had visited in that time; now, 450 years later, years during some of which the Abbey had been profoundly critical of the papacy, the moment would come. The service would of course be carefully planned, but I thought it might not be easy. It had to be fully ecumenical, representing and including a complete cross section of the Christian communities in England, Wales and Scotland, and yet the Archbishop of Canterbury must have a leading role as Primate of All England. The historic independence from episcopal authority of the Abbey as a Royal Peculiar needed to be honoured without our looking self-important. The choral tradition of the Church of England needed to have a prominent place, without the Anglican tradition of worship being seen as an exercise in archaism. Purely practically, if the Pope had been some time in Westminster Hall, he might need a small break at the Abbey before the service proper began. I was determined that the visit should start appropriately at the Grave of the Unknown Warrior.

Two precedents were in my mind. I retained a memory of the historic moment when Archbishop Michael Ramsey visited Pope Paul VI in Rome in 1965. The two prelates were seated, their chairs half turned to face each other, in front of the altar of the Sistine Chapel and Michelangelo's *Last Judgement*, each wearing choir dress, Pope Paul in white soutane and skull cap with a rochet, mozzetta and stole, and Archbishop Ramsey in cassock, rochet, chimere and scarf, with his purple velvet Canterbury cap. Michael Ramsey's cap remained in my mind. The other precedent in my mind was the visit of the Ecumenical Patriarch, Bartholomew I, to the Abbey for Evensong with the Archbishop of Canterbury in January 2007. He was in London to celebrate the signing of the first report of the Anglican/Orthodox dialogue *The Church of the Triune God*. At the end of Evensong, the patriarch and the archbishop had prayed together at the Shrine of St Edward and jointly censed the tomb. On that occasion I had recalled that the Great Schism between the western and eastern churches, between Rome and Constantinople, had occurred during the life of St Edward.

Planning for the papal service had to be conducted with several partners. We had enormous help in identifying the various churches, Christian communities and ecumenical groupings that should make up the congregation. The Abbey's protocol department and IT staff worked hard to produce a means by which these groups could receive a general invitation and then invite their chosen representatives to register at a dedicated website; this would both allow final invitations to be sent out without further manual intervention and also furnish for police vetting a comprehensive list of those planning to attend.

None of us knew how the papal visit would be received in Great Britain. The media were full of antagonism. Some officials at the Foreign and Commonwealth Office had been reported to have made critical jokes about the Roman Catholic Church. The Vatican's response to issues around clerical abuse of children remained highly controversial. There were the usual questions about the cost of the visit and in this case about the division of responsibility for the budget between the government and the Roman Catholic Church. Prominent atheists were opportunistic in raising their voices against the Church. The mood changed, though, when the Pope arrived in Scotland, to meet the Queen at Holyroodhouse Palace, and was welcomed by enthusiastic crowds lining the streets of Edinburgh. As so often, a sceptical media, hedging their bets, had failed to predict the national mood.

The service began with the congregation assembled in good time for them to be able to watch the Pope's address in Westminster Hall. They saw the popemobile travel around Parliament Square and were amused by the site of protection officers running with the vehicle and children being snatched from the crowd to be presented to the Holy Father. Finally Pope Benedict XVI arrived to cheers from the crowd outside the Abbey heavily muffling the small sounds of protest. He was accompanied by the three archbishops, of Canterbury, York and Westminster, in cassocks. I had decided to greet him in cassock and gown at the west gate. This was an unusually significant welcome. Normally the Dean only greets at the gate the Queen or whoever is the senior member of the Royal Family attending a particular service, generally receiving even the most distinguished visitors at the Great West Door. Protocol sometimes allows the stretching of convention – and it seemed right.

It also gave me an important opportunity. As I led the Pope towards the Great West Door, I pointed out some of the twentieth-century martyrs commemorated in stone on the west front of the Abbey, especially Dietrich Bonhoeffer and Maximilian Kolbe. I also indicated the statue of Oscar Romero, Archbishop of San Salvador.

On the 30th anniversary in March 2010 of Oscar Romero's assassination at the altar, we had held a special Sunday evening service attended by the Archbishop of Westminster and his predecessor, Cardinal Cormac Murphy-O'Connor, at which the Archbishop of Canterbury gave the address. The ambassador of El Salvador, a relation of Oscar Romero, was present. I had written to an earlier ambassador at the suggestion of Canon Anthony Harvey to object to a proposal in El Salvador that the politician who ordered the archbishop's assassination should receive an official pardon. On that occasion I was surprised to receive an impromptu visit by the Vice-President of El Salvador accompanied by journalists and photographers and a camera crew. She took me aside, after I had given her a brief tour of the Abbey and we had been filmed looking at the statue, to tell me that the government had no plans to implement the proposal. The pause to see the statue as the Pope entered the Abbey was I understand seen as it happened in El Salvador. Oscar Romero's brother, I was told, wept.

Entering the Abbey itself, I led Pope Benedict to stand at the east end of the Grave of the Unknown Warrior. I greeted him:

> Your Holiness, the Dean and Chapter welcomes you most warmly as the first Pope to visit this Church dedicated to St Peter, which has been the kingdom's coronation church since 1066, and which, for 600 years as a Benedictine Abbey, until the English Reformation, enjoyed a close relationship of mutual support with the papacy. Heads of State visiting Her Majesty The Queen join us here in respect for the Grave of the Unknown Warrior, since 1920 a potent symbol, for this nation and for the world, of the suffering and devastation of warfare. I invite you to lead us in asking of almighty God, for his world and for his people, the gift of peace.

The prayer I had proposed the Pope should use had been written by Eric Milner-White, sometime Dean of King's College Cambridge and then of York, who had also devised the form for the Festival of Nine Lessons and Carols. It was a prayer for peace. You will find it at the end of this chapter.

I then presented to the Pope the senior representatives of the Christian communities of the British Isles, who were lined up on the south side of the Grave. We retired to the Jericho Parlour to vest, while the choir sang a series of anthems. The ecumenical representatives processed to the Sacrarium. The final anthem was a setting in English, by the sixteenth-century composer, a Roman Catholic tolerated by Elizabeth I, Thomas Tallis, of words from St John's Gospel, Chapter 15: 'If ye love me, keep my commandments. And I will pray the Father, and he shall give you another Comforter, that he may bide with you for ever; even the Spirit of truth.'

The Pope and Archbishop accompanied by the Dean and Chapter emerged from the Jericho Parlour and waited on the south side of the nave for the collegiate procession to form.

The choir sang an invitatory composed by Gabriel Jackson, a commission for the service, which finished with a magnificent sense of joy with resounding Alleluias.

V. The glory of the Lord has risen upon us.

R. Let us rejoice and sing God's praise for ever.

Glory to the Father and to the Son and to the Holy Spirit;

as it was in the beginning is now and shall be for ever. Amen.

Alleluia.

The play-over began for the processional hymn *Christ is made the sure foundation*. I turned to His Holiness and pointed out that the tune had been written by Henry Purcell. He was Organist of the Abbey from the age of 20 in 1679 to his death in 1695; by the Pope's reaction, I judged that he knew of Purcell and his music but not of his connection with the Abbey. Here, as in so much else, the Pope showed evident delight and interest in the whole experience. After the service he asked me to send him some CDs of the Abbey choir.

Now in the Sacrarium, at chairs in front of the high altar, partly turned to face each other, the Archbishop and Pope greeted one another and exchanged the Kiss of Peace. The Archbishop greeted the Pope on behalf of all British Christians, before presiding at the office of Evening Prayer:

YOUR Holiness, brothers and sisters in Christ:

On behalf of the Christian communities of Great Britain, we welcome you in fraternal love to this great shrine, which has been of such significance for both Church and nation.

For many centuries the daily Office of the Church has been celebrated here, first by Benedictine monks, then by the new foundation of the sixteenth century, always with the same rhythms of psalmody and petition, and the same purpose of glorifying God in all things.

As we join now in that unbroken tradition, we pray that our *sacrificium laudis* – our sacrifice of praise – will become more and more a sign of the sacrificial love which we offer together in Christ's name for the renewal of our society and our whole world in the power of his Spirit.

May your visit be a blessing for all who share with you in pilgrimage and discipleship.

His Holiness Pope Benedict XVI responded. I was particularly touched by his recognition of the continuing influence of the Christian Gospel on the culture of England and also by the humility of his coming to the tomb of St Edward as a pilgrim:

YOUR Grace, Mr Dean, dear friends in Christ,

I thank you for your gracious welcome. This noble edifice evokes England's long history, so deeply marked by the preaching of the Gospel and the Christian culture to which it gave birth. I come here today as a pilgrim from Rome, to pray before the tomb of Saint Edward the Confessor and to join you in imploring the gift of Christian unity. May these moments of prayer and friendship confirm us in love for Jesus Christ, our Lord and Saviour, and in common witness to the enduring power of the Gospel to illumine the future of this great nation.

A version of Evening Prayer began with Psalm 138 sung to Anglican chant and continued with a reading given by Dame Mary Tanner:

Let the same mind be in you that was also in Christ Jesus, who, though he was in the form of God, did not regard equality with God as something to be exploited, but emptied himself, taking the form of a slave, being born in human likeness. And being found in human form, he humbled himself and became obedient to the point of death – even death on a cross. (Philippians 2: 5–8; NRSV)

The Moderator of the General Assembly of the Church of Scotland read Mark 10: 43–45 again about servant leadership quoting the words of our Lord Jesus Christ:

You know that among the Gentiles those whom they recognise as their rulers lord it over them, and their great ones are tyrants over them. But it is not so among you; but whoever wishes to become great among you must be your servant, and whoever wishes to be first among you must be slave to all. For the Son of Man came not to be served but to serve, and to give his life a ransom for many.

The Pope and the Archbishop venerated St Augustine's sixth-century Gospel book, preserved at Corpus Christi College Cambridge, and then each gave an address.

The Pope remembered that 2010 'marks the hundredth anniversary of the modern ecumenical movement, which began with the

Edinburgh Conference's appeal for Christian unity as the prerequisite for a credible and convincing witness to the Gospel in our time.' He went on to recall 'the remarkable progress made toward this noble goal through the efforts of committed Christians of every denomination' and the challenge 'in a society which has become increasingly indifferent or even hostile to the Christian message.' We must 'proclaim with renewed conviction the reality of our reconciliation and liberation in Christ, and propose the truth of the Gospel as the key to an authentic and integral human development.' The Church's unity, he said, 'can never be other than a unity in the apostolic faith'.

> Dear friends, we are all aware of the challenges, the blessings, the disappointments and the signs of hope which have marked our ecumenical journey. Tonight we entrust all of these to the Lord, confident in his providence and the power of his grace. We know that the friendships we have forged, the dialogue which we have begun and the hope which guides us will provide strength and direction as we persevere on our common journey. At the same time, with evangelical realism, we must also recognise the challenges which confront us, not only along the path of Christian unity, but also in our task of proclaiming Christ in our day. Fidelity to the word of God, precisely because it is a true word, demands of us an obedience which leads us together to a deeper understanding of the Lord's will, an obedience which must be free of intellectual conformism or facile accommodation to the spirit of the age. This is the word of encouragement which I wish to leave with you this evening, and I do so in fidelity to my ministry as the Bishop of Rome and the Successor of Saint Peter, charged with a particular care for the unity of Christ's flock.

The Archbishop recalled the influence of St Gregory in bringing the Gospel of Jesus Christ to England and the inspiration of St Benedict:

In St Gregory's Dialogues, we can trace the impact of St Benedict – an extraordinary man who, through a relatively brief Rule of life, opened up for the whole civilization of Europe since the sixth century the possibility of living in joy and mutual service, in simplicity and self-denial, in a balanced pattern of labour and prayer in which every moment spoke of human dignity fully realised in surrender to a loving God. The Benedictine life proved a sure foundation not only for generations of monks and nuns, but for an entire culture in which productive work and contemplative silence and receptivity – human dignity and human freedom – were both honoured.

He spoke of 'the dehumanising effects of losing sight of Benedict's vision':

We live in an age where there is a desperate need to recover the sense of the dignity of both labour and leisure and the necessity of a silent openness to God that allows our true character to grow and flourish by participating in an eternal love.

The Archbishop acknowledged the contribution the Pope had made to re-establishing 'a Benedictine vision for our days':

And in this, we are recalled also to the importance among the titles of the Bishops of Rome of St Gregory's own self-designation as 'servant of the servants of God' – surely the one title that points most directly to the example of the Lord who has called us. There is, we know, no authority in the Church that is not the authority of service: that is, of building up the people of God to full maturity. Christ's service is simply the way in which we meet his almighty power: the power to remake the world he has created, pouring out into our lives, individually and together, what we truly need in order to become fully what we are made to be – the image of the divine life. It is that image which the pastor in the Church seeks to serve, bowing down in reverence before each human person in the knowledge of the glory for which he or she was made.

The choir sang the Magnificat to Charles Villiers Stanford's setting in A, during which I censed the altar, and then the Pope, the Archbishop and the other church leaders. After prayers led by young people of the Roman Catholic Church in England and Wales and of the Church of England, the Collect and the Lord's Prayer, the Pope and Archbishop joined me in prayer at the Shrine of St Edward and offered incense at the tomb. The Archbishop prayed for the public life of our countries to be strengthened by the Christian vision of the kingdom of God and the Pope prayed for Christian unity.

Before giving the Blessing, the Pope and Archbishop together venerated the high altar with a kiss, the Pope taking the initiative. This sign of papal respect for an Anglican altar took me by surprise and delighted me. As the service concluded and the procession moved west through the Abbey church, the congregation burst into prolonged applause. It was an extraordinary moment, a spontaneous outburst of joy and a sign of hope, a sign of reconciliation.

It is impossible to tell what will be the fruits of that joint prayer and ecumenical witness. It was certainly an occasion of deep prayer and proclaimed harmony but it would have been mistaken to expect any immediate pronouncements or particular steps. There will be fruits, not just of this service of Evening Prayer but of the whole papal visit. One fruit will be renewed confidence in maintaining the strength of the tradition of Christian witness to the Gospel in the nation. That is already apparent from within the Roman Catholic community. At the end of his visit, the Pope set his encouragement to the Roman Catholic bishops to promote the Ordinariate for former Anglicans within two particular aspects of the context. The first was the need for the Catholic Church to receive from the Anglican tradition something of its particular patrimony. The second was the ultimate goal, still there, reiterated by the Pope explicitly, of full visible Christian unity, in fidelity to the prayer of our Lord the night before he died that 'they might all be one, that the world might believe' (John 17). One thing was clear for all to see that evening. The Pope is a man of personal piety and humility. He may lack the personal magnetism of his predecessor John Paul II. But these evident characteristics are powerful and attractive in themselves in one holding such prominent office. And he seemed genuinely to enjoy his experience of worshipping almighty God within the Anglican tradition in Westminster Abbey, at the heart of our national life.

In the light of the terrible conflict between Catholics and Protestants over the centuries and still now in parts of the world, and of the violence and terror unleashed within our own national life in the past by Catholics against Protestants and by Anglicans against Catholics, this was an authentic moment when the fruits of the Holy Spirit were in evidence, above all the fruit of reconciliation and of peace.

I offer you here the prayer for peace uttered by the Pope at the beginning of his visit to Westminster Abbey:

LORD God, you hold both heaven and earth in a single peace. Let the design of your great love shine on the waste of our anger and sorrow, and give peace to your Church, peace among nations, peace in our homes, and peace in our hearts; in Jesus Christ our Lord. Amen.

8

The Royal Maundy

'The fruit of the Spirit is love, joy, peace, forbearance, kindness, generosity, faithfulness, gentleness and self-control' (Galatians 5: 22).

Kindness

A hundred years and more ago it had become customary to think of Westminster Abbey as our National Mausoleum. That is understandable. Arthur Penrhyn Stanley (Dean of Westminster from 1864 to his death in 1881) had sought to awaken the Abbey from the gentle somnolence that had fallen on it in the latter half of the eighteenth century and which had survived into the reign of Queen Victoria. To be fair, Samuel Wilberforce (Dean 1845), son of William Wilberforce, was an energetic and creative man, but he was in post all too briefly before becoming successively Bishop of Oxford and Winchester, where he found himself in bitter argument with Huxley about Darwin's theory of evolution and earned the soubriquet Soapy Sam. William Buckland (Dean 1845–1856), a noted zoologist, spent most of his time at Islip in Oxfordshire, where the Dean and Chapter hold the rectory, and is said not to have visited the Abbey for ten of his twelve years as Dean. Richard Chenevix Trench (Dean 1856–1864) by contrast had

introduced a Sunday Evening Service 'for the local poor', in the Nave–
its first use for many a long year – before he became Archbishop of
Dublin, a post he is said to have hated.

One means by which Stanley could develop the Abbey as a national
institution was to introduce statues of statesmen. We see them in the
north transept: three Cannings, Peel, Palmerston; after Stanley, Dis-
raeli looking one way, Gladstone the other. No more, was the cry, once
the Grand Old Man, Gladstone, was in place. But it was all too much
for some critics. At the turn of the last century, there was a plan developed to build a new national mausoleum, linked to the Abbey's south-
east corner and stretching along Millbank. It would have been vast,
and distinguished by a tower half as tall again as the Victoria Tower
at the southern end of the Palace of Westminster. All the monuments
would have been removed from the Abbey to what was dubbed the
new national Valhalla. Plans were abandoned partly because William
Morris and his Society for the Protection of Ancient Buildings criti-
cized the damage to the Abbey through the proposed link between
the buildings, though they would have been delighted no doubt at
the opportunity to see again the clear Gothic lines of the medieval
building.

So the Abbey remains the place of burial or memorialization of
3,300 people, dating from the earliest times to the present. There are
abbots and monks, deans and canons, receivers general and chapter
clerks, surveyors and clerks of the works, minor canons and organists,
headmasters of Westminster School, former pupils, statesmen, archi-
tects, musicians, poets, authors, actors, scientists, diplomats, explor-
ers, spies, soldiers, sailors and airmen, benefactors and activists. We
still add to the number of memorials from time to time. The latest

is a ledger stone to the Poet Laureate Ted Hughes in Poets' Corner. It is difficult to know whom to include and whom to exclude. Once they are there, they are there for ever, the remembered and the long-forgotten. Oddly, almost every Prime Minister of the first half of the twentieth century is buried or memorialized in the Abbey, but none since Clement Attlee, an omission to my mind not easily explained. Here you can find the history not only of England and the United Kingdom and of the Commonwealth, but of our whole civilization, the English-speaking world.

But the Abbey is not just about history. I long for the million and more visitors who enter as tourists during the day through the Great North Door (probably unaware that this was the old royal entrance to the Abbey) to have a sense, not only of this great history but also of the Abbey as a working church, that places above all things in importance the daily worship of almighty God and the fulfilling of its ancient Christian mission to proclaim the power and beauty and love of God to the world. We decided fairly early in my time as Dean to replace the audio guide with one that would allow the visitor to delve deeper and discover something of the religious meaning of the parts of the Abbey they were seeing: the font in the Lady Chapel, which was moved decades ago from what is now St George's Chapel in the south-west corner of the nave; the high altar; the quire. Jeremy Irons kindly volunteered to spend a day recording the English version. Some time later we decided, since only 20% of the visitors were paying the extra charge for the audio guide, to adjust the entrance charge so that the audio guide would be an automatic part of the package. We have just added a version in Korean, the twelfth language. The Abbey is much quieter now during visiting hours and we hope our visitors are better informed. The duty chaplains, who are available to the visitors for advice, information and 'sacramental ministry' and also lead a minute's prayer from the pulpit every hour, now also bring anyone who wishes from among the visitors at 11 and 3 into the Shrine of St Edward for pilgrim prayers. We also welcome parish pilgrim groups visiting almost every Wednesday evening and hold an annual pilgrimage on the Saturday after the feast of the Translation of St Edward the Confessor in October.

For the Abbey clergy, the heart of our life is the daily office and the Eucharist and the weekly and yearly rhythm of the Abbey's worship. We are all together as far as possible on a weekday morning for Morning Prayer at 7.30 in St Faith's Chapel at the southern end of the south transept. The chapel was only brought into use for prayer a hundred years ago, after beginning life as a sacristy and for centuries after the Dissolution being a place for general storage; its lack of decoration makes it a refreshing change from the rest of the Abbey church and an appropriate place for the early morning. We are almost always joined by a handful of others, some regulars, some early visitors who have learnt from a tourist guide or website that this is a time of free admittance if only you will pay the price of prayer. The Eucharist is at 8 every day of the year, except of course at the end of Holy Week, sometimes in St Faith's Chapel, sometimes in the Shrine of St Edward, or the chapel of the Holy Name or St George's or the Pyx chapel or, for the feasts of our Lord or our Lady, the Lady Chapel, and at 12.30 on a weekday at the nave altar. Except on a Wednesday when it is said, Evensong is sung every day, by the Abbey choir in term, on alternate Mondays by the Choristers or the Lay Vicars, for part of the school holiday by the Lay Vicars, and for the rest of the time by usually fine visiting choirs from around the world. On Sunday, the pattern is Holy Communion at 8, Choral Matins at 10, Sung Eucharist at 11.15, Choral Evensong at 3 with a visiting preacher, organ recital at 5.45 and Evening Service, no longer in the nave but in the lantern and transepts, at 6.30. It is a rich diet and supports all the manifold activity of the day and the week.

The annual rhythm includes the celebrations of St Peter our patron and St Edward the Confessor in June and October, but is based, as in every church, around the great feasts of Christmas and Easter, which, with the solemn celebration of the Three Holy Days, Maundy Thursday, Good Friday and Holy Saturday, focus our minds on the central tenets of the Christian faith: that God loves so much the world as part of the universe he has created that he comes to share our life as a human being, to teach us and give us an example by which to live, to suffer and to die for us and to rise again to new life. He, who came not to serve but to be served and to give his life as a ransom for many, shows us that self-giving love is the only way to happiness. The great services of Maundy Thursday, Good Friday and Holy Saturday night are fully celebrated in the Abbey. In 2011 for the first time in many years, there had been an adult confirmation preparation class, with candidates due to join the choirboys' confirmation on the Sunday before St Peter's Day. And pupils from Westminster City School and Grey Coat Hospital, church schools with a strong local connection to the Abbey, were to be confirmed by the Bishop of London at the Westminster School confirmation service. A number of members of these two groups had not been baptized, so it was a great joy for me to baptize them at the Paschal Vigil. Another candidate for the Abbey confirmation, baptized the evening before, was Peter who had been

converted and received the gift of the Christian faith while attending an Abbey Sung Eucharist in January 2011. Such events are truly
heartening, since we have little real evidence about how the many
hundreds or thousands attending Abbey services are touched. We
pray and trust that, as long as we play our part as conscientiously as
possible, the Holy Spirit of God will reach and change people. But it is
good sometimes to hear the stories.

On Maundy Thursday at the Eucharist of the Last Supper, the
Canon in Residence and I wash the feet of twelve members of the
congregation, as our Lord washed his disciples' feet. There was quite
a sensation in the media when Rowan Williams reintroduced that
practice at Canterbury Cathedral in his first year as archbishop. But
generally the media have not been keen to give attention to the Royal
Maundy, an ancient tradition, still lively, whereby the Sovereign follows the example of the Saviour in re-enacting the foot-washing. In
truth, it would be sensational if the Queen actually washed the feet
of those whom she was honouring. It is in any case powerful that the
Queen, following the example of her predecessors over many centuries, year by year honours with a symbolic gesture elderly people who
have followed the example of our Lord, in giving their lives to the
service of the Church and community.

The Queen has only missed the Royal Maundy service twice in her
long reign. Her father George VI was also very loyal to the service,
which nevertheless, until the reign of George V, had not been conducted personally by the Sovereign for centuries. In medieval times
and until modern times, the Royal Maundy ceremony took place
wherever the king or queen happened to be. Later, the Sovereign was
represented by a senior courtier. The Queen decided early in her reign

that the ceremony should move around from county to county and from cathedral to cathedral in the United Kingdom. Once in recent years the Royal Maundy was conducted at the cathedral of the Archbishop of Armagh, the Primate of All Ireland. Following the Queen's coronation, the ceremony was at first conducted at the Abbey every other year and then every fourth year but since 1981 it has been with us every tenth year. In 2010, I wrote to invite the Queen for the 2011 service and was pleased that the invitation was accepted, especially since her 85th birthday on 21 April would fall that day. I would certainly have hoped the service would be at the Abbey, even had I known that eight days later we would be celebrating the marriage of Prince William and Catherine Middleton, the Duke and Duchess of Cambridge.

It was agreed that the Abbey's extended community would provide half the recipients, with the other half coming from two dioceses of the Church of England that would never expect to be able to host the ceremony: the diocese of Sodor and Man, being too small (covering no more than the Isle of Man), and the diocese of Europe, being too big (with a cathedral in Gibraltar and pro-cathedrals in Brussels and Valletta).

I decided that we would find the names of the Abbey's 85 recipients from among former Abbey staff and volunteers, regular worshippers, the parishes where the Abbey appoints the incumbent (Abbey livings) and the parishes of Abbey priests vicar and duty chaplains. We also invited our ecumenical neighbours and friends, Westminster Cathedral and Westminster Central Hall, to provide some names.

The Royal Almonry is responsible for the planning of the service with the Abbey and the Lord Chamberlain's Office. The Secretary of the Royal Almonry produced a note of the history of the Royal Maundy for the order of service:

Today's 801st known Royal Maundy Service is very special as it falls on The Sovereign's birthday and this year the Bishop of Sodor and Man, the Bishop of Gibraltar in Europe, together with the Dean of Westminster have been invited to nominate Maundy Recipients. Thus people from England, the Isle of Man and across Europe make up the eighty-five men and eighty-five women who will receive their Maundy Gifts from The Queen on Her Majesty's eighty-fifth birthday.

The distribution of Alms and the washing of the feet on the Thursday of Holy Week are of great antiquity. The Maundy can be traced back in England with certainty to the twelfth century, and there are continuous records of the Distribution having been made on Maundy Thursday from the reign of King Edward I. The first known Royal Distribution from records we have at present was at Knaresborough, North Yorkshire by King John in 1210.

The Service derives its name from the Latin word mandatum, meaning a commandment, and its opening words are, 'Jesus said: "I give you a new commandment."'

From the fifteenth century, the number of recipients has been related to the years of the Sovereign's life. At one time recipients were required to be of the same sex as the Sovereign, but since the eighteenth century they have numbered as many men and women as the Sovereign has years of age. Recipients are now pensioners selected because of the Christian service they have rendered to the Church and the community. The Distribution is in two parts, and the gifts which are handed to the recipients are symbolic.

The red purse contains an allowance for clothing and provisions formerly given in kind and a payment for the redemption of the royal gown. The white purse contains in Maundy coins silver pennies, tuppences, threepences and fourpences, as many pences as the Sovereign has years of age. Maundy coins are legal tender, and when the United Kingdom changed to decimal currency in 1971, the face value of a set of four coins became 10 new pence, instead of 10d in the old £sd system.

Though the act of washing the feet seems to have been discontinued in about 1730, the Lord High Almoner and his assistants are still girded with linen towels in remembrance, and carry the traditional nosegays of sweet herbs.

In earlier times the Ceremony was observed wherever the Sovereign was in residence. For many years the Maundy Gifts were distributed in the old Chapel Royal (now the Banqueting Hall) in Whitehall, but from 1890 to 1954 the Service was held at Westminster Abbey, except during the Coronation years of 1937 and 1953 when the Service took place at St. Paul's Cathedral. This year will mark the sixteenth occasion the Service has been held at Westminster Abbey during the present Reign.

The Lord High Almoner is always a diocesan bishop, currently Nigel McCullough, Bishop of Manchester, and is assisted by clergy and officials from the Royal Household. The Choir of Her Majesty's Chapels Royal sings with the choir of the church hosting the service. The Roman Catholic Archbishop of Westminster and the Greek Orthodox Archbishop Gregorios of Thyateira and Great Britain, both of whom are well-established friends of the Abbey, were ecumenical representatives at the service.

The service has a well-established pattern, beginning with John Henry Newman's hymn *Praise to the holiest in the height* from *The Dream of Gerontius*, with its verses so appropriate to Holy Week:

> O generous love! that he, who smote
> in Man for man the foe,
> the double agony in Man
> for man should undergo;
> And in the garden secretly,
> and on the Cross on high,
> should teach his brethren, and inspire
> to suffer and to die.

After opening versicles and responses, as at Matins, and a Psalm, prayers were said that reflected on the humility of our Lord in washing the disciples' feet and the wish that this act should itself set an example for others to follow.

> LORD Jesus Christ, who before instituting the Holy Sacrament at thy Last Supper, washed the feet of thine Apostles: teach us, by thine example, the grace of humility: and so cleanse us from all stain of sin that we may worthily partake of thy holy mysteries; who with the Father and the Holy Spirit art one God, world without end.

For the first distribution, the Queen walked the length of the south side of the Abbey, down the nave and east again to the south transept, distributing the purses, carried on great dishes by Yeomen of the Guard, to the first 85 recipients. The congregation, including the Duke of Edinburgh, remained standing throughout. The Duke then read a lesson, St Matthew's account of the Last Judgement:

JESUS said: 'When the Son of Man comes in his glory and all the angels with him, he will sit in state on his throne, with all the nations gathered before him. He will separate people into two groups, as a shepherd separates the sheep from the goats, and he will place the sheep on his right hand and the goats on his left. Then the King will say to those on his right hand, "You have my Father's blessing; come, enter and possess the kingdom that has been ready for you since the world was made. For when I was hungry, you gave me food; when thirsty, you gave me drink; when I was a stranger you took me into your home, when naked you clothed me; when I was ill you came to my help, when in prison you visited me." Then the righteous will reply, "Lord, when was it that we saw you hungry and fed you, or thirsty and gave you drink, a stranger and took you home, or naked, and clothed you? When did we see you ill or in prison, and come to visit you?" And the King will answer, "I tell you this: anything you did for one of my brothers here, however humble, you did for me." Then he will say to those on his left hand, "The curse is upon you; go from my sight to the eternal fire that is ready for the devil and his angels. For when I was hungry, you gave me nothing to eat, when thirsty, nothing to drink; when I was a stranger, you gave me no home; when naked, you did not clothe me; when I was ill and in prison you did not come to my help." And they too will reply, "Lord, when was it that we saw you hungry or thirsty or a stranger or naked or ill or in prison, and did nothing for you?" And he will answer, "I tell you this: anything you did not do for one of these, however humble, you did not do for me." And they will go away to eternal punishment, but the righteous will enter eternal life.' (Matthew 25: 31-46; NEB)

The second distribution then took place on the north side of the Abbey, while again the choirs sang anthems, concluding with Handel's coronation anthem *Zadok the priest*. After further prayers and the General Thanksgiving and the seventeenth-century hymn *My song is love unknown* by Samuel Crossman, the service concluded with the Lord's Prayer, a final prayer, the National Anthem and the blessing.

Following the service, the Queen met children from local schools in Dean's Yard, including the children of the Abbey choir, and was given flowers as the children sang Happy Birthday. It all presented a pretty picture, with the Queen beaming.

The particular fruit of the Spirit that I have chosen to identify with this special service is kindness. Like gentleness, this might seem soft and easy. But I think that is misleading. It would be far better for the world and for everyone if more of us were willing recipients of this fruit of the Spirit. Kindness is not a soft option. It is not the same as not being unkind. It requires us to intend actively to be kind, to reach out in generosity and love, and without being patronizing. The new commandment of our Lord to his disciples on this day of all days, the eve of the Lord's Passion, is to reach out in kindness, in generosity and love. We find it in Chapter 13 of St John's Gospel:

> You call me "Master" and "Lord", and rightly so, for that is what I am. Then if I, your Lord and Master, have washed your feet, you also ought to wash one another's feet. I have set you an example: you are to do as I have done for you.

This act of kindness offers us a real challenge, a difficult example to follow. I hope many of those who watched the service on 21 April

2011, as well as those of us who participated in it, will have had a chance to reflect on this truth.

There were many delights associated with the service. One of the recipients, quite elderly, had never before left the Isle of Man. One intended recipient had died just a few days before the service, but his closest relations were invited to receive the Maundy money on his behalf. Following the service and a reception in the Jerusalem Chamber, attended by the Queen and Duke, the Abbey gave a lunch in Church House for the recipients and their closest family supporter. It was a delightful occasion and an amazing preparation for the wonders of the Triduum, the three great holy days. Some colleagues from the Abbey and I now habitually attend the Bishop of London's Chrism Eucharist in St Paul's Cathedral, at which the oils are blessed for the sacraments of the sick, of initiation and of ordination, and priestly vows are renewed. We renewed our priestly vows after Morning Prayer that morning quite quietly in St Faith's Chapel.

During the ceremony, the choirs sang a beautiful setting by Johannes Brahms of these words by the seventeenth-century poet Paul Flemming. I hope you find it helpful for meditation.

GEISTLICHES LIED

LAß dich nur nichts nicht dauern mit Trauern, sei stille,
Wie Gott es fügt, so sei vergnügt mein Wille!
Was willst du heute sorgen auf morgen? Der Eine
Steht allem für, der gibt auch dir das Deine.
Sei nur in allem Handel ohn' Wandel, steh' feste,
Was Gott beschleußt, das ist und heißt das Beste. Amen.
Do not be sorrowful or regretful, be calm,

as God has ordained, so my will shall be content!
What do you want to worry about from day to day?
There is One who stands above all, who gives you too what is yours.
Only be steadfast in all you do, stand firm,
what God has decided, that is and must be the best. Amen.

This prayer from the Royal Maundy ceremony might also inspire your own prayer and action. It was read by the Archbishop of Westminster, Vincent Nichols:

ALMIGHTY God, our heavenly Father, who hast given thy Son Jesus Christ to die for our sins, and hast commanded us to love one another as thou hast loved us: make us, we beseech thee, so mindful of the needs and suffering of others, that we may ever be ready to show them compassion and, according to our ability, to relieve their wants; for the sake of the same Jesus Christ our Lord, who liveth and reigneth with thee, in the unity of the Holy Spirit, one God, world without end. Amen.

9

The Royal Wedding

'The fruit of the Spirit is love, joy, peace, forbearance, kindness, generosity, faithfulness, gentleness and self-control' (Galatians 5: 22).

Love

When I was a parish priest I generally enjoyed the occasional offices: baptisms, weddings and funerals. I think most clergy appreciate the opportunities such ministries offer them of reaching out beyond their particular congregation. Closely involved with people at important moments in their lives, you can share the mysteries at the heart of our faith about God's creative and nurturing love and about his triumph in his Son over the powers of sin and death. Funerals can, of course, sometimes be difficult and painful, as on one particular occasion I remember following the accidental death of a child. They can also be fruitful in developing relationships and bringing people into connection with the Church. You find so often that people are genuinely open to questions of faith but have rarely had the opportunity to even consider them as applied to their own lives. In a large parish, these ministries will often be time-consuming but can also be refreshing.

They are a privilege for the clergy of the Church of England and an important part of what I heard the Bishop of Leicester call, in a discussion with parliamentarians in the Jerusalem Chamber, 'Establishment on the ground'.

Establishment is a privilege for the Church of England. It is not the privilege of dominance but of service. When I was the Church of England's chief education officer, one of the fiercest critics of Christianity and the Church, the journalist Polly Toynbee, engaged with me in a brief discussion on BBC Radio 4's *Today* programme. We were both in the Westminster studio talking 'down the line' to Sue McGregor in the main studio at White City. The subject was something to do with church schools or Religious Education. As we left the studio together, Polly Toynbee turned to me and said: 'The Church of England does three things well: weddings, funerals and church schools. Why don't you make more of them?' Precisely what I am trying to do, I thought. But by then her attention was drawn to Tam Dalyell, still then a Member of Parliament, wandering into the studio no doubt for his own three or four minutes on the air.

During my seventeen years in parishes, I must have conducted many hundreds of these occasional offices, a ministry I missed in my fourteen years in the Church's education service. So it was a surprise and pleasure when I discovered that Westminster Abbey, both the Abbey church itself and St Margaret's Church within the precincts, has its own ministry in baptisms, weddings and funerals. Neither the Abbey church nor St Margaret's has any parochial responsibilities. St Margaret's was a parish church, with a parish that included Downing Street, though the Dean and Chapter of Westminster always appointed the Rector from among their own number. In 1972, an Act of Parliament, not contested by the Abbey, changed the relationship, depriving St Margaret's Church of its parish and making it simply part of the Abbey.

While the Abbey is not a parish, the Dean and Chapter understand ourselves as having at least a degree of pastoral responsibility for those living within the Abbey precincts. That includes the Palace of Westminster and Westminster School as well as the Abbey's Choir School. The pastoral responsibility will involve occasional baptisms and weddings and, though only rarely, funerals. St Margaret's Church is seen as the parish church of parliament. Members of Parliament, both in the House of Commons and the House of Lords, are often happy to have occasional offices celebrated for themselves and members of their immediate families in St Margaret's Church or in the Chapel of St Mary Undercroft within the Palace. Memorial services are a significant part of the work of St Margaret's. Famously, at the end of the Second World War, the Prime Minister, Winston Churchill, led Members of Parliament across the road to St Margaret's Church for a service of thanksgiving. At the beginning of the new Parliament in 2010, a well-attended service in St Margaret's was arranged with the Parliamentary Christian Fellowship.

The Abbey's Lady Chapel, built at the expense of Henry VII in the first decade of the sixteenth century in perpendicular Gothic style replacing Henry III's thirteenth-century Lady Chapel, and which became the place of his burial, has since 1725 also been the chapel of the Order of the Bath. George I revived the Order, which had previously been awarded in association with coronations but had been in abeyance for some years. George III expanded the Order and now it is awarded in military and civil divisions and at three levels: Companion,

Knight Commander or Dame Commander and Knight Grand Cross. The highest level is in practice awarded to the heads and most senior members of the armed services and the most senior civil servants, outside the Foreign and Commonwealth Office whose diplomats are honoured within the Order of St Michael and St George. The red sash of the GCB is familiar from the portraits of Horatio, Lord Nelson at his death. Companions, with CB after their name, are themselves all senior civil or military servants. Members of the Order of the Bath have the privilege for themselves and their children of marriage in the Lady Chapel and for their children and grandchildren of baptism there. The privilege of services in the Lady Chapel does not extend beyond their death, with the exception of memorial services for GCBs after the banner has been removed from their stall in the Chapel.

Generally funerals at the Abbey are very rare. Seventeen kings and queens regnant are buried in the Abbey, in several cases with their queen, or in the case of Queen Anne, prince, consort: St Edward the Confessor; Henry III; Edward I; Edward III; Richard II; Henry V; Edward V, murdered in childhood in the Tower with his brother the Duke of York; Henry VII; Edward VI; Mary I; Elizabeth I; James I; Charles II; Mary II and William III; Anne; George II. For five hundred years therefore, most of the kings and queens of England, and then also of Scotland and of the United Kingdom, were buried in the Abbey. Since George III's in 1820, royal funerals and burials have taken place at Windsor Castle. Queen Elizabeth The Queen Mother's funeral in 2002 was at the Abbey, though she is buried with George VI in St George's Chapel Windsor.

The case of royal weddings is different. There were six at the Abbey in the Middle Ages including those of Henry I and Richard II but none thereafter until the twentieth century. In the nineteenth century, Queen Victoria's wedding was at the Chapel Royal, St James's Palace, and that of her son, Edward VII, when he was Prince of Wales, and her grandson, George V, as Duke of York, at St George's Chapel Windsor. In the twentieth century, the Abbey again became the normal choice, following the wedding of Princess Patricia of Connaught in 1919. Princess Mary, later the Princess Royal, the only daughter of George V and Queen Mary, was married in 1922, George VI when he was Duke of York married Lady Elizabeth Bowes-Lyon in 1923, then the Duke of Kent (the father of the present Duke) married Princess Marina and, as we already know, the Queen when she was Princess Elizabeth married the Duke of Edinburgh in 1947. Princess Margaret was married at the Abbey in 1960, Princess Alexandra in 1963 and Princess Anne in 1974. The Prince of Wales' marriage to Lady Diana Spencer at St Paul's Cathedral was an exception to the twentieth-century pattern. The last twentieth-century royal wedding at the Abbey was that of Prince Andrew, Duke of York in 1986. Prince Edward, Earl of Wessex, and Sophie Rhys-Jones were married in 1999 at Windsor.

When the engagement was announced on 16 November 2010 between Prince William of Wales and Miss Catherine Middleton, there was some press speculation about where the wedding would take place. It was suggested that it might be comparatively low key at Windsor or indeed almost completely private at the Chapel Royal, which seats 100 people. We had no prior warning of the announcement, which had been kept splendidly secret, and had no idea whether the Abbey would be the choice. Speculation mounted the following day, when it was reported that Catherine Middleton had made a private visit to the Abbey. Not so private, since pictures were published in the papers, taken perhaps from a phone camera, of the bride-to-be leaving the cloister entrance, establishing a pattern for almost every visit of the couple or their best man and bridesmaids to the Abbey, despite the best endeavours of their protection officers. For several days or even weeks before the wedding, photographers were in attendance at the entrances to Dean's Yard.

Catherine Middleton's first visit was a pleasant occasion, relatively brief, involving a walk through the Abbey, but we had no clear indication whether she was happy that the wedding should be there. When it was announced the following Tuesday on 23 November that it would be at the Abbey on 29 April, it was reported that the choice was made because of the Abbey's 'stunning beauty', its 1,000-year royal history and its 'surprising intimacy'. The date of 23 November was already a special day for the Abbey, since the Queen with the Duke of Edinburgh was attending a Sung Eucharist, to be followed by a ceremony in Church House Westminster for the inauguration of the General Synod of the Church of England at the beginning of its new quinquennium. The announcement was made during the service. Instead of attending the inauguration as planned, I made myself available for a long series of interviews with the media. I said that the most important point for me was that this wedding, like any other, must be powerfully personal for the couple. I hope I also made it clear that the wedding must reflect the central truth of marriage as a celebration of God's gift of love. I looked forward to the detailed planning for the wedding. For excellent reasons, it was all to happen within a comparatively short time span. The wedding would be on the Friday after Easter, a busy time in the life of any church, and particularly so with the Royal Maundy on the Thursday before Easter. Anzac Day, an important part of the annual calendar of the Abbey, would be com-memorated with a large service on Easter Monday.

Coordination was of course vital in the planning. The Abbey was represented on the St James's Palace planning group. There was an Abbey planning group, involving all the key departments in the Abbey, that reported directly to me. I had my own meetings with the couple to talk about the order of service itself and they also met more than once Dr Rowan Williams, Archbishop of Canterbury, who would solemnize the marriage, and Dr Richard Chartres, Bishop of London, who would give the address and who, as a university friend of the Prince of Wales, had been a spiritual counsellor to Princes William and Harry. He had confirmed Prince William as a schoolboy, and confirmed Catherine shortly before the wedding. The couple were well supported but all the key decisions were their own. They wanted everyone to enjoy the day and for it to be a proper celebration. The Prime Minister announced that it would be a public holiday.

I think we had little idea at the time of the announcement what the level of public interest would be. The BBC eventually reckoned that the television audience was the largest of any event in the history of broadcasting, with 2.2 billion people watching, about a third of the world's population. Many of the world's television stations wanted access to the Abbey in the first three months of 2010, and our communications team worked very hard to keep to a minimum the disruption to the Abbey's routine and to our visitors. The BBC was very helpful in sharing footage of the work in progress. In London, as the various media villages went up, anticipation increased. Well ahead of the wedding itself the crowds were beginning to grow opposite the Abbey and along the processional route. Following the great services of Holy Week and Easter, the heart of the Church's Year, celebrated with the normal full solemnity and ceremony and attended by very large congregations (on Easter Day 7,500 people at five services), and the Anzac Day service at 9 o'clock on Easter Monday, the Abbey was open to visitors just for two days and closed for preparations from Wednesday. The trees, the field maples that would line the nave and two hornbeams to frame the Sacrarium, were brought in on Wednesday evening. For a time we wondered whether their arrival could be kept secret for the day, but that would have been impossible in practice. So the media were invited in.

Final rehearsals took place: with the couple; with Prince Harry, the best man, Pippa Middleton, the bride's sister and maid of honour, and the bridesmaids; with James Middleton, Catherine's brother, who read the lesson. Her parents, Michael and Carol Middleton were staunch in their support. A final run-through for the BBC, attended by the bride's father with stand-ins for Prince William and Catherine, must have felt very strange for Michael Middleton.

One of the key tests at those rehearsals had been how the various musicians involved would be able to get the balance and tempo of each piece of music just right, with the choir of the Abbey and the choir of the Chapels Royal in the quire stalls, the London Chamber Orchestra on the quire screen and fanfare trumpeters on scaffolding high up to the north and south of the quire. The broadcasters' help, with a camera trained on James O'Donnell and a loud-speaker beside him conveying the sound of the orchestra, and a TV screen in the loft, made everything possible. Without the skill and effective collaboration of the various directors, none of it would have worked. In the event, it all seemed perfect.

After the rehearsals on Thursday evening, the red carpet was laid, work being finished at 2 o'clock in the morning. Our clerk of the works and his team, who had supervised the rigging of the Abbey and the introduction of the trees and flowers and so much more besides and who remained in attendance, would have to appear again in time for the final security check at 6 am. No doubt many of us felt quite apprehensive on the evening before the wedding. I wandered through the Abbey as the activity began to die down, initially to check that everything was as it should be and to think through my own role. I found myself in the Shrine of St Edward and then in the Lady Chapel and its north and south aisles, with their royal tombs. I felt the intimacy of the Abbey and its warmth on that occasion and I can only describe the sensation, as my wandering turned into prayer, of the history of the Abbey and its mission as a House of God and House of Kings rising up to embrace this young royal couple about to embark on a most remarkable experience, at the centre of the world's attention for the duration of the wedding ceremony, and then in the world's spotlight for the whole of their earthly life together. The next morning at 6.30, I was at prayer in my oratory, the Abbot's Pew, with its balcony overlooking the west end of the nave of the Abbey. At 7, with one of the Abbey choristers, Theo Beeny, I did a television interview for the BBC at the media village opposite the Abbey. At 7.30, I was in St Faith's Chapel for Morning Prayer with the Abbey clergy and celebrated the Eucharist there at 8, praying for God's blessing on the day and on the couple. At 8.30, I had a good breakfast and at 9 was out with the Canons meeting the crowds near the Abbey. From 9.30, we were at the Great West Door and the congregation was already beginning to fill the Abbey Church. The process was under way. The wonderful Abbey

team and so many associated with us in the planning and preparation, the great human machine, moved forward, serene and certain.
Standing at the Great West Door greeting people as they arrived, I had
a strong feeling of the happiness of the occasion somehow rendering
any sense of nervousness pointless.

Princes William and Harry arrived at 10.15 so that they could
have informal conversations with some of the guests before retir-
ing to St Edmund's Chapel for a time of preparation and waiting.
The last members of the Royal Family to arrive were the Prince
of Wales and Duchess of Cornwall, followed, a few minutes later,
by the Queen and the Duke of Edinburgh, whom I greeted at the
west gate. I led them to their places on the south side of the lantern
and then returned to the west end to await the arrival of first the
bridesmaids and then – a breath-taking moment – the bride with
her father. When the dress was settled and all was still, I turned to
start the bridal procession and then began the great music for the
entrance of the bride, Sir Hubert Parry's well-known and loved setting of psalm 122, first used at the coronation of Edward VII in 1902
and, as we have seen, sung at the coronation of the present Queen
in 1953.

> I was glad when they said unto me: We will go into the house of
> the Lord.
> Our feet shall stand in thy gates: O Jerusalem.
> Jerusalem is builded as a city: that is at unity in itself.
> O pray for the peace of Jerusalem: they shall prosper that love
> thee.
> Peace be within thy walls: and plenteousness within thy palaces.

After the hymn *Guide me O thou great Redeemer* had been sung to the Welsh tune *Cwm Rhondda*, and the couple were ready at the prayer desks at the west end of the Sacrarium, I stepped forward to read the Bidding. The couple had chosen an order of service using the traditional language, first prepared, as an adaptation of the 1662 order for Holy Matrimony, for the 1928 prayer book, which was never approved by parliament but published nevertheless and widely used, and which was much more recently authorized by General Synod for permanent use. The bidding sets out the reasons for marriage:

> Dearly beloved, we are gathered here in the sight of God, and in the face of this congregation, to join together this man and this woman in Holy Matrimony; which is an honourable estate, instituted of God himself, signifying unto us the mystical union that is betwixt Christ and his Church; which holy estate Christ adorned and beautified with his presence, and first miracle that he wrought, in Cana of Galilee, and is commended in Holy Writ to be honourable among all men; and therefore is not by any to be enterprised, nor taken in hand, unadvisedly, lightly, or wantonly; but reverently, discreetly, soberly, and in the fear of God, duly considering the causes for which Matrimony was ordained.
>
> First, It was ordained for the increase of mankind according to the will of God, and that children might be brought up in the fear and nurture of the Lord, and to the praise of his holy name.
>
> Secondly, It was ordained in order that the natural instincts and affections, implanted by God, should be hallowed and directed aright; that those who are called of God to this holy estate, should continue therein in pureness of living.

Thirdly, It was ordained for the mutual society, help, and comfort, that the one ought to have of the other, both in prosperity and adversity.

Into which holy estate these two persons present come now to be joined.

Therefore if any man can shew any just cause why they may not lawfully be joined together, let him now speak, or else hereafter for ever hold his peace.

When the Archbishop of Canterbury had addressed the couple asking them too whether there was any impediment to their marriage, the Solemnization of the Marriage began with the promises and vows and the blessing and giving of the wedding ring. When the bride said 'I will' in the Abbey it was possible to hear the cheer of the crowd listening to the broadcast outside and to see a delighted smile cross the face of the bridegroom. This stage of the service continued with the prayer of the Archbishop:

O Eternal God, Creator and Preserver of all mankind, giver of all spiritual grace, the author of everlasting life: Send thy blessing upon these thy servants, this man and this woman, whom we bless in thy name; that, living faithfully together, they may surely perform and keep the vow and covenant betwixt them made, whereof this ring given and received is a token and pledge; and may ever remain in perfect love and peace together, and live according to thy laws; through Jesus Christ our Lord. Amen.

Then, the Archbishop joined their hands and bound them with the ends of the priestly stole around his neck and said, 'Those whom God hath joined together let no man put asunder' and announced the marriage. He concluded with a blessing for the couple:

> God the Father, God the Son, God the Holy Ghost, bless, preserve, and keep you; the Lord mercifully with his favour look upon you; and so fill you with all spiritual benediction and grace, that ye may so live together in this life, that in the world to come ye may have life everlasting. Amen.

The congregation sang Charles Wesley's hymn *Love divine, all love's excelling,* to the Welsh tune *Blaenwern,* that has become so closely associated with it in recent years. The lesson was read by James Middleton, from Romans 12: 1–2 and 9–18, and the choirs sang a newly commissioned anthem by John Rutter to texts from the psalms, chosen by the composer and approved by the couple:

> This is the day which the Lord hath made: we will rejoice and be glad in it.
> O praise the Lord of heav'n: praise him in the height.
> Praise him, all ye angels of his: praise him, all his host.
> Praise him, sun and moon: praise him, all ye stars and light.
> Let them praise the Name of the Lord.
> For he shall give his angels charge over thee: to keep thee in all thy ways.
> The Lord himself is thy keeper: the Lord is thy defence upon thy right hand;
> so that the sun shall not burn thee by day: neither the moon by night.
> The Lord shall preserve thee from all evil: yea, it is even he that shall keep thy soul.

The Lord shall preserve thy going out and thy coming in: from this
time forth for evermore.

He shall defend thee under his wings.

Be strong, and he shall comfort thine heart, and put thou thy trust
in the Lord.

The Bishop of London, Dr Richard Chartres, then gave the address,
which I include in full:

"Be who God meant you to be and you will set the world on fire."
So said St Catherine of Siena whose festival day this is. Marriage
is intended to be a way in which man and woman help each other
to become what God meant each one to be, their deepest and their
truest selves.

Many people are fearful for the future of today's world but the
message of the celebrations in this country and far beyond its
shores is the right one – this is a joyful day! It is good that people
in every continent are able to share in these celebrations because
this is, as every wedding day should be, a day of hope.

In a sense, every wedding is a royal wedding with the bride and
groom as king and queen of creation, making a new life together so
that life can flow through them into the future.

William and Catherine, you have chosen to be married in
the sight of a generous God who so loved the world that he gave
himself to us in the person of Jesus Christ.

In the Spirit of this generous God, husband and wife are to give
themselves to each other.

Spiritual life grows as love finds its centre beyond ourselves.
Faithful and committed relationships offer a door into the mystery

of spiritual life in which we discover this: the more we give of self, the richer we become in soul; the more we go beyond ourselves in love, the more we become our true selves and our spiritual beauty is more fully revealed. In marriage we are seeking to bring one another into fuller life.

It is of course very hard to wean ourselves away from self-centredness. People can dream of such a thing but the hope will not be fulfilled without a solemn decision that, whatever the difficulties, we are committed to the way of generous love.

You have both made your decision today – "I will" – and, by making this new relationship, you have aligned yourselves with what we believe is the way in which life is spiritually evolving, and which will lead to a creative future for the human race.

We stand looking forward to a century which is full of promise and full of peril. Human beings are confronting the question of how to use wisely the power that has been given to us through the discoveries of the last century. We shall not be converted to the promise of the future by more knowledge, but rather by an increase of loving wisdom and reverence, for life, for the earth and for one another.

Marriage should transform, as husband and wife make one another their work of art. It is possible to *trans*form so long as we do not harbour ambitions to *re*form our partner. There must be no coercion if the Spirit is to flow; each must give the other space and freedom. Chaucer, the London poet, sums it up in a pithy phrase:

"Whan maistrie [mastery] comth, the God of Love anon,
Beteth his wynges, and farewell, he is gon."

As the reality of God has faded from so many lives in the West, there has been a corresponding inflation of expectations that personal relations alone will supply meaning and happiness in life. This is to load our partner with too great a burden. We are all incomplete: we all need the love which is secure, rather than oppressive. We need mutual forgiveness in order to thrive.

As we move towards our partner in love, following the example of Jesus Christ, the Holy Spirit is quickened within us and can increasingly fill our lives with light. This leads on to a family life which offers the best conditions in which the next generation can receive and exchange those gifts which can overcome fear and division and incubate the coming world of the Spirit, whose fruits are love and joy and peace.

I pray that all of us present, and the many millions watching this ceremony and sharing in your joy today, will do everything in our power to support and uphold you in your new life. I pray that God will bless you in the way of life you have chosen, that way which is expressed in the prayer that you have composed together in preparation for this day:

> God our Father, we thank you for our families; for the love that we share and for the joy of our marriage. In the busyness of each day keep our eyes fixed on what is real and important in life and help us to be generous with our time and love and energy. Strengthened by our union help us to serve and comfort those who suffer. We ask this in the Spirit of Jesus Christ. Amen.

The choir sang as a Motet, a setting by Paul Mealor of the words *Ubi caritas* from I John 4: 'Where charity and love are to be found, God is there.' After prayers and William Blake's hymn *Jerusalem*, set to music by Sir Hubert Parry and arranged by Sir Edward Elgar, I said a final prayer and pronounced the blessing.

During the signing of the registers, which took place in the Shrine of St Edward, *Blest pair of sirens* was sung, John Milton's apostrophe to the pledges of heaven's joy, Voice and Verse, to Parry's music, culminating in a clear vision of our eternal destiny in heaven: 'O may we soon again renew that song, and keep in tune with heaven, till God ere long to his celestial concert us unite, to live with him, and sing in endless morn of light.'

After a fanfare, incorporating the RAF call, the orchestra played William Walton's *Crown Imperial*, written for the 1937 coronation, as the couple slowly left the Abbey followed by the maid of honour and best man, the bridesmaids, the Prince of Wales and Duchess of Cornwall and Michael and Carol Middleton. Finally, I led the Queen and the Duke of Edinburgh to the west gate for the carriage processions to Buckingham Palace.

At the Abbey we received many messages of congratulation and felt a great sense of satisfaction. There was some media interest in the cartwheel in the Nave of one of the vergers, caught on camera when the Abbey was empty and broadcast without authorization. There was some speculation that he might have been disciplined. Far from it! He expressed physically the sense of delight and exuberance we all felt emotionally. There was also media interest in the two religious sisters in the Sacrarium in their grey-green habits. They were our chaplain Sister Judith of the Community of the Sisters of the Church, accompanied by Sister Annaliese CSC who assists regularly with the chaplaincy work. They were sitting in their normal place. Nor to my knowledge is either of them working for the Security Service.

Love is the fruit of the Spirit I have chosen in relation to this service. Above all, we were celebrating the love of God and his gift of himself to this young couple in love. From the beginning I hoped and intended that this would be seen not as an extraordinary but as an exemplary service, reminding us all, participants and congregation, viewers and commentators alike, of the centrality of Christian marriage to the life of our society and world. I hope still that it will have been an encouragement to others as they think of their relationship and of marriage, and also to those undergoing difficulties in their lives together.

God's gift of love, his creative, generous power, is what makes us what we are and keeps us who we are. That is surely God's whole purpose in the creation of the universe, the world and of us human beings: that we might love him and each other for his sake. I conclude with a prayer from the service, which you might like to make your own for the young couple and those you know and love:

O God, who hast taught us that it should never be lawful to put asunder those whom thou by Matrimony hadst made one, and hast consecrated the state of Matrimony to such an excellent mystery, that in it is signified and represented the spiritual marriage and unity betwixt Christ and his Church: look mercifully upon these thy servants, that both this man may love his wife, according to thy Word (as Christ did love his spouse the Church, who gave himself for it, loving and cherishing it even as his own flesh), and also that this woman may be loving and amiable, and faithful to her husband, and in all quietness, sobriety, and peace, be a follower of holy and godly matrons. O Lord, bless them both, and grant them to inherit thy everlasting kingdom; through Jesus Christ our Lord. Amen.

10

Servant Leaders:
A way of life

'The fruit of the Spirit is love, joy, peace, forbearance, kindness, generosity, faithfulness, gentleness and self-control' (Galatians 5: 22).

We all exercise influence on those around us, in our family circles, among our friends, at school, college or work, in our community. It is not only politicians and commentators, heads of major corporations, fashion icons, world-famous sports personalities, heads of government and heads of state who are leaders. We are all leaders. Our leadership should not be one of dominance but of service: not dictators but servant leaders.

Our natural instincts, deep within us, incline us to want our own way, to manipulate others to our own ends, to put ourselves first. However hard we try, these instincts keep reasserting themselves. It is only by constant or repeated openness to the grace of God, to the gifts of the Holy Spirit, God working within us through prayer, study of his Word, recourse to the sacraments, that this deep instinct to selfishness can be overcome. In the end, that is not our work, but God's work in us.

I began writing this in that part of France, between the rivers Dordogne and Garonne south of the Gironde estuary, called Entre Deux Mers, surrounded by miles and miles of vines. There has been sunshine and rain. I have scarcely seen a farmer or heard a tractor. The long lines of vines mostly have their grapes hanging low beneath the leaves. It is only August but they are beginning to look luscious and full. No doubt there will be much hard work and business at the time of the grape harvest which may be early this year, in September. But now it seems that the vines, like the seed in our Lord's parable, grow by themselves.

> Jesus also said, 'The kingdom of God is as if someone would scatter seed on the ground, and would sleep and rise night and day, and the seed would sprout and grow, he does not know how. The earth produces of itself, first the stalk, then the head, then the full grain in the head. But when the grain is ripe, at once he goes in with his sickle, because the harvest has come.' (Mark 4: 26-29; NRSV)

We have been thinking about how we may nurture the fruits of the Spirit in ourselves. We should be encouraged by the thought of the vines to recognize that these fruits are the gift of God, not of our own work or achievement, not to be striven for, but allowed by God's good grace to grow in us, through our being increasingly open to the love of God in our own lives.

We have more especially thought about how we may hold these fruits of the Spirit up to view in our lives, thus encouraging others to seek the virtues and values that have made our world civilized. In that context I have given some account of the public ministry exercised at

Westminster Abbey and thereby, I hope, given you some access to its life and mission.

One of the driving ideas for the Dean and Chapter's mission at the present moment is about giving access. That means several things. We want to give our visitors better access to the Abbey's significance not only as a historic monument, a national mausoleum, a place of stunning beauty, but as a House of God, where almighty God has been worshipped day after day for a thousand years and where the worship of almighty God continues to be understood as genuinely possible, really important and indeed vital to enabling us to be the people God wishes us to be.

We would also like our visitors to understand how closely interwoven the history of the Abbey has been with our national life. The geography itself is significant, so close to the legislature, the executive and the judiciary. The Abbey is to the south of Parliament Square, on whose north-hand side stands HM Treasury and HM Customs and Revenue, to the west the Supreme Court and to the east the Houses of Parliament themselves in the historic royal Palace of Westminster. This geographical significance is not just historic. It is not simply that the Church has had – the Gospel of Jesus Christ has had – a significant impact on our national life. The Abbey continues to characterize the contemporary relevance of the Church's mission and ministry.

Another part of giving access is opening up more parts of the Abbey to our visitors. We are as I write converting the *Cellarium*, the monastic cellar, a fourteenth-century part of the Abbey buildings facing on to Dean's Yard, into a restaurant on two floors, the upper floor yielding extraordinary views of the Abbey and of the Victoria Tower of the Palace of Westminster. This will allow visitors for the first time to have a really interesting place where they can sit down in comfort for a meal or a cup of coffee. We shall also be able to clear the Great Cloister for the first time for many decades of all that prevents people experiencing it as the wonderfully reflective space it was always intended to be.

Then we plan to open up the eastern part of the Triforium, the great space half way up to the ceiling which runs all around the Abbey Church itself. That will offer wonderful views inwards to the Church below and outwards to the Palace of Westminster. There we shall be able to display far more of the Abbey's treasures than can be shown in the current museum, itself for the past hundred years in the eleventh-century Undercroft in the Dark Cloister, one of the most interesting parts of the Abbey buildings. The Undercroft will then itself be available for the purpose of showing the visitor more of the contemporary life and mission of the Abbey.

The Abbey's life, I hope I have shown, is much more than the daily and weekly round of worship, central and vital though that is; much more than welcoming the million or so visitors a year who come as tourists and, we hope, leave as pilgrims; much more than working to give them a better experience. We are striving all the time to be of service, open to connections and links, to collaboration with other Christians, with those of other religions, with men and women of goodwill, networks of all kinds, along which we can carry the message of Christian faith at the heart of our national life, faith in the nation.

On 16 November 2011, there is to be a service in the Abbey – will have been by the time you read this – to celebrate the 400th anniversary of the publication of the Authorized Version, the King James Bible. This is not simply to be a celebration of the remarkable initiative of James I and the work of the translators, but of the influence on the nation and on the English-speaking world of the Bible in English.

On Christmas Day 2010, in her television broadcast to the nation and the Commonwealth, the Queen began with a reference to the anniversary. She was speaking from Hampton Court, one of the historic royal palaces. The Queen said:

> Over four hundred years ago, King James the Sixth of Scotland inherited the throne of England at a time when the Christian Church was deeply divided. Here at Hampton Court in 1604, he convened a conference of churchmen of all shades of opinion to discuss the future of Christianity in this country. The King agreed to commission a new translation of the Bible that was acceptable to all parties. This was to become the King James or Authorized Bible, which next year will be exactly four centuries old.
>
> Acknowledged as a masterpiece of English prose and the most vivid translation of the scriptures, the glorious language of this Bible has survived the turbulence of history and given many of us the most widely-recognised and beautiful descriptions of the birth of Jesus Christ which we celebrate today.
>
> The King James Bible was a major cooperative endeavour that required the efforts of dozens of the day's leading scholars. The whole enterprise was guided by an interest in reaching agreement for the wider benefit of the Christian Church, and to bring harmony to the Kingdoms of England and Scotland.

I love that last phrase 'agreement for the Church and harmony for the kingdoms' which sees the influence of the Church as being fundamental to the good estate of the realm.

The year 2011 has seen an extraordinary range of initiatives in connection with the Bible quatercentenary, promoted by the initiative of
the Bible Society, from broadcasts and lectures, to exhibitions and
performances, to the publication of books. A particularly interesting
book has been written by Melvyn Bragg identifying and praising the
cultural and religious influence of the King James Bible, with a touch
of nostalgia for something that has almost been lost. Though Lord
Bragg himself is clear that he cannot share the fullness of the Christian faith as understood by the Church of England, nevertheless he
acknowledges its influence for good.

Professor Grace Davie has written extensively on the current religious scene and described the attitude of many people in Britain and
Europe today as *believing but not belonging*. In practice, believing
comes from belonging. Faith has to be nurtured within the religious
context or it will be a poor and puny thing. The powerfully symbolic
acts of worship I have described and the strong liturgical, musical and
cultural tradition in the Abbey can, I believe and trust, provide a context in which those many thousands of people every week who join us
in worship can be nurtured in the Christian faith and in their spiritual
lives, can advance a little further along the path towards God, or, to
change the image, delve deeper into the inner reality of their own lives
to find the God who is the very ground of their being.

Faith is not a matter of intellect. We do not have to understand to
believe. Indeed, faith comes first. St Anselm in the eleventh century
speaks of faith seeking an understanding: *credo ut intelligam*. I believe
in order that I might understand. The fourteenth-century author of

The Cloud of Unknowing says of God that he 'can well be loved, but he cannot be thought. By love he can be grasped and held; but by thought neither grasped nor held.' He advises how to approach this task: 'Beat continually upon this cloud of unknowing that is between you and your God with a sharp dart of longing love.'

Michael Ramsey, after his retirement as Archbishop of Canterbury, gave the addresses at the retreat I attended in the diocese of Southwark before I was made deacon on St Peter's Day 1975. I remember him then telling us that there would be times – perhaps not many – when we could truly say we loved God. We should thank God for those times. There would be others when at least we knew we really wanted to love God. We should thank God for those, too, and God could do something with that. But there would be other times when we could not say we wanted to love God but could say we really wanted to want to love God. God could do something with that. And there would be other times when even that was too much for us, but we could at least say that we wanted to want to want to love God. God could even do something with that.

If we are able to recognize our deep human need to love God and that it is from that love that will flow our love of our neighbour, then we are in the process of becoming nurtured in the faith and formed into the likeness of our Lord Jesus Christ, the Son of Man, who came 'not to be served but to serve and to give his life a ransom for many' (Mark 10: 45). Like him, we shall be enabled to become servant leaders, exercising influence for good in those fellowships and communities of which we are part.

The Common Worship Collect for Trinity 9 is a fitting summary of all the prayers:

Almighty God, who sent your Holy Spirit to be the life and light of your Church; open our hearts to the riches of your grace, that we may bring forth the fruit of the Spirit in love and joy and peace; through Jesus Christ our Lord. Amen

POSTSCRIPT

During my first five years at the Abbey, I have been mightily blessed through the collaboration with inspiring and helpful colleagues.

Becoming Dean of Westminster is daunting but I received unfailing encouragement and support from my first Receiver General, Major General David Burden CB CVO CBE, as I have from his successor, Sir Stephen Lamport KCVO DL. Working with them has been instructive and enjoyable. Without them the Abbey machine would grind to a halt. In close and vital support too is my Personal Assistant Dr Non Vaughan-O'Hagan. Stephen and Non have both read drafts of this book and made helpful comments, though they bear responsibility neither for the book itself nor for errors of judgement or fact.

To have had three Sub-Deans in five years has had nothing to do with carelessness; all three, together with the other Canons, who with me make up the Dean and Chapter of Westminster, the Abbey's governing council, have been wise and thoughtful colleagues. I am grateful to them all: Robert Wright, Nick Sagovsky, Bob Reiss, Jane Hedges, Andrew Tremlett and Vernon White.

The major work in planning the Abbey's many special services falls on the Minor Canons: in my time Graeme Napier, Deiniol Morgan, Michael Macey, Ralph Godsall and Jamie Hawkey. James O'Donnell, Organist and Master of the Choristers, with Robert Quinney, Sub-Organist, and their colleagues in the music department bring the highest skill and professionalism to the work as well as a deep commitment to the worship of almighty God. The other key Abbey department in planning these events has been Protocol, now part of Event Management: Stuart Holmes MVO, Matthew Arnoldi, Colonel Julian Lyne-Pirkis, Wing Commander Jules Eaton, Tony Platt and John Wright, working with the Chief Honorary Steward Roger Westbrook and his excellent team of volunteers. I thank them all.

Collaborators outside the Abbey are far too many to name here. The Abbey's close working relationships with Lambeth Palace and the Royal Households are highly valued. The staff of the BBC have been unfailingly co-operative and professional.

So many others have the power to make an event run smoothly or not: Martin Castledine, the Dean's Verger, and his colleagues; the marshals led by Peter Crook and now Alex Anderson; Jim Vincent, Clerk of the Works and his team; the yard beadles and attendant cleaners. They deserve warm thanks, as do so many other members of the Abbey community it would be impossible for me to acknowledge within the scope of these few words.

I have learnt a great deal about the Abbey from John Burton, Professor Warwick Rodwell, Dr Tony Trowles and Dr Richard Mortimer. Duncan Jeffery and his communications team, for whom many of these particular services have involved special demands unfailingly met, have been helpful in identifying photographs for the book, as has Christine Reynolds.

The High Steward and High Bailiff hold important honorary positions as advisers within the collegiate body. The Rt Hon The Lord Hurd of Westwell CH CBE and his successor as High Steward The Rt Hon The Lord Luce KG GCVO have been real friends to the Abbey and to its Dean. Sir Roy Strong, besides offering his commitment of generous friendship and support, has added to our collective knowledge of the history of the Abbey and of our nation through his book *Coronation*, published by Harper Collins in 2005, which was immensely helpful to me in the preparation of the chapter in this book on the Coronation. Any inaccuracies in my chapter are, needless to say, entirely my own fault.

Caroline Chartres suggested I write a book and encouraged me with the proposal for this book. I am grateful for her enthusiasm and support and to her colleagues at Bloomsbury.

I thank the Most Revd and Rt Hon Dr Rowan Williams and the Rt Revd and Rt Hon Dr Richard Chartres KCVO for permission to include quotations from addresses they have given in the Abbey and to Sir Andrew Motion and his successor as Poet Laureate, Carol Ann Duffy, for permission to reproduce their own works read in services at the Abbey.

INDEX